An Endless Travel

A complete planning document
to turn post retirement life
into joy and peace

An Endless Travel

A complete planning document to turn post retirement life into joy and peace

Dewakar Goel

BANYAN TREE BOOKS PVT. LTD.
7/31, Ansari Road, Daryaganj, New Delhi-110 002

First Edition : 2010
Second Edition : 2015
Price : Rs. 250
$ 12

Published by
Banyan Tree Books Pvt. Ltd.
(Rajkamal Prakashan Group)
7/31, Ansari Road, Daryaganj
New Delhi-110 002 (India)
email : info@rajkamalprakashan.com
Website : www.rajkamalprakashan.com

Cover Design : Deba Jyoti Datta (Dev)

Printed at
B.K. Offset
Naveen Shahadara, Delhi-110 032

ISBN: 978-81-905401-5-5

A tribute to my parents
Shri Daya Prakash Goel and Smt. Vinay Goel
Whose planned life remained
The source of inspiration to pen this book

End of one journey

For beginnging of another

"Life is an endless & triumphant journey
Into the realms of emotional stability
The maturity to realise unfulfilled enjoyment and
Dreams to nurture the passion
Gives time for reinventing oneself"

Preface

Planning is a natural activity for any human being whether he is in childhood or in the youth or leading towards maturity. In every walk of life, one needs to plan for years ahead.

The title of this book *An Endless Travel* symbolises that during our whole life, we are in different phases. We cannot confine planning for retirement only since it goes beyond touching various aspects of life.

My endeavour is to propagate the message "We never retire."

It is only our mindset which makes us old. Otherwise, if we are keeping healthy body, there is no reason to feel for retirement.

The planning for old age is quite an important aspect in a number of foreign countries. My experience of visiting European and Asian countries reveals that people have made this planning process as a business when they solicit nomination of the people in old age to join them for learning various activities which may be helpful for a planned retired life. In India, I could not find a single book which addresses this issue. Well, old age homes are everywhere maybe to exploit the situation to their advantage as a business.

I hesitate in using the word 'retirement' mainly because of the reason that word retirement gives quite negative connotations.

While writing this preface, I want to inform my readers that as a first step of growing in age it is essential to recognise the need to have emotional and psychological stability. Since our expectations, sensibilities, personalities, sensitivity level, perception, concept of empathy all undergo a sea change.

Therefore, when we grow old to have "superannuation" from the regular service, before entering to next phase of working life, we must prepare for emotional and psychological changes in our thinking process.

In every chapter of this book, I have illustrated real life situations and tried to relate and analyse the situations. I had interaction with the people who played roles in real life as narrated by me in these stories. As a matter of fact, my idea is not only to generate awareness, but also to justify the particular planning. The emphasis is given as to what wrong happens when a person does not go for a particular planning. You will find the chapters dedicated to financial, health and legal planning where one needs to devote time and energy. Otherwise, the life will become a burden. The idea is to enjoy each phase of life as it comes and not to think about ageing process.

Look at the chapter on "Matrimony?" Which may be looking quite strange in Indian context, but it is a reality that a person may look for a partner in old age when children get settled and wife departs for heavenly abode, then where to go for emotional security. Nobody has time for that person. Just think what is wrong if, like in a movie a person comes across as his life partner in the similarly placed situation. Well, I think a marriage of the widower with a widow is not a bad idea.

Spirituality is not a new subject for us. Nowadays even a management graduate is being taught spiritual values for various management techniques. I have taken a separate chapter which relates to spirituality giving peace of mind. I had to take inputs from our *Vedas* and other religions. I do not intend to make this as a religious book, but definitely, I feel it should touch the human values.

The subjects included in this book are having universal application and do not confine to a particular age group mainly because when you are reading the stories, you will find persons how they lived in a particular phase of life and if you debate on ifs and buts followed by now, why, when and what, then it will give you a real insight. Especially, when you feel like wearing a particular shoe, to know as to where it pinches.

Every writer feels that his writings are the best for readers and I am no exception. I am confident that this book will prove as landmark not only as a guide for the people to plan their second or third phase of life but also a rare collection of stories for the younger generation giving them a new vision, a new field, a new direction for serious thinking.

With the above words, I look forward for the opinion from my readers in the form of not only suggestion, but also criticism in analytical manner which will be welcomed for giving food for thought and motivation to cover untouched aspects in the next edition of this book.

—Dewakar Goel

Dewakar Unleashed

Professor Dewakar Goel, the multi-faceted personality is a top administrator on one hand and an excellent philosopher on the other. As an administrator he has always been performance driven, on the other had as a philosopher, he has always tried to find out the socio-economic causes that prompt human being to very ruthless acts at times. When a commoner gets into a rickshaw, he only thinks of reaching the destination, but the inquisitive eyes of charismatic Dewakar always penetrates the shell of rickshaw puller to find out his whereabouts and even he wants to realise his problems during the journey.

We can hardly deny that high level of aspirants and indomitable desire of human beings to achieve even unachievable due to the rat race of today's globalisation causes stress, strain and stretch, which become difficult for many to fathom. Here comes the role of a real friend, philosopher and guide like Dewakar, who has done his Ph.D. in stress management and is continuously invited from many countries to talk on stress due to his overwhelming capabilities of analyzing stress, strain and stress caused by today's competitive world and its wide spread impact on people of various segment.

Dewakar, a management scholar with a simultaneous experience in teaching and officiating in top position for more than two decades, was invited by Asian Airports Summit 2008 at Singapore as chairperson and speaker, was the only Indian to talk on **"Influence of Stress on Performance of Aviation Sector Across the World"**. He is being invited quite frequently as the chairperson and speaker for international conferences, his forthcoming visits are for Malaysia to talk on "360 degree appraisal" and then he is scheduled to deliver a talk on "contract labour system" in Singapore.

When the philanthropic characteristics of human beings hide behind the self-propelling characteristics, Dewakar is very keen to re-synthesizing the morale even in such a competitive world. Dewakar believes life is a journey on endless road with certain milestones, having flowers and thorns too. So, why to lose the normal rhythm in small twists? Success and failures, both are part of life only. People can surely bear with stretch as rewarding professionalism demands stretched endeavours from people at times. The problem comes up when you become envious of others without comparing your strengths and weaknesses, which cause an additional strain in your mindset and get reflected through your entire appearance and behaviour.

The human nature is so fragile that a little glory at times earns so much pride that one tends to forget the reality. At times even a slightest deviation in your dreams or plans leads you to take drastic decision. The success for the orator Dewakar is not destined but it is a journey on unknown road. We must understand that the life is much larger than term in true in sense than a mere success and failure, and we must not forget to step down to earth. The philosopher Dewakar gives an excellent example; life is like a circle moving across the axis...where movement is life. We all have a spot to measure years of life by counting the rounds that moving circle makes across the axis, whenever it touches that spot a good or bad happening occurs you to get associate with those who help in improving the motion of circle. The life is happy if there is no break no friction...the smooth movement is happiness.

How Dewakar can achieve such admirable success in human behaviour? Perhaps his specialisation in labour law from Indian Law Institute and his vibrant presence in Delhi Court as an advocate have allowed him to intrude into the various types of crimes of human beings. His specialisation in Personnel Management and Industrial Relations has paved the way to come much closer to the Human Relation problems and prompted him to innovate solutions, which he has been able to test on various people in his professional endeavours. *Performances Appraisal and Compensation Management*, published by Prentice Hall of India, is an excellent textbook on personnel management and it gives a different outlook of modern management to the students community. Dewakar believes learning is a continuous process and to prove what he believes, he has specialised in the field of "Instructional Technology" from IATA, Geneva, Switzerland to acquire the rare distinction of being the only IATA qualified Indian instructor to train Aviation Personnel across the world in Human Resource discipline. It is the passion for mankind, which drives the philosopher Dewakar to the success path.

Dewakar's eyes sparkle, when he is asked to reveal the secret of success, it is the high-rise, which is purely based on some ethics of life like honesty, integrity, dedication, determination and passion. His fight against corruption has become a legend among many youngsters. The author Dewakar had created a ripple in Delhi Book Fair, 2000 for his book on departmental enquiries co-authored with advocate wife Sangeeta and published by JAICO. The most important part is he hardly gets fatigued even after running so many activities throughout the day. He is also a poet, a singer, an author, a professor and a strong administrator. Dr. Dewakar feels that every professional has got the opportunity of keeping marks, whether in private sector or public sector, if and only if he is serious and sincere to his profession. Perhaps Javed Akhtar in Kolkata Book Fair, 2001 has brought him into the limelight as a poet. Leaps and bounds, still he maintains contacts with each and really becomes responsive and impulsive for any of their needs as he feels friendship is real property which can never face any depreciation.

At some corner of his very private world, Dewakar feels the existence of the Almighty and his controlling nature, life is the creation of supernatural power what we say God and what you meet in life is fixed, it has to happen, what may come but how you feel it is not fixed it is in your hand, you are free to cry or laugh...on happenings. We believe this is a very natural phenomenon for a philosopher like Dewakar, who is a life member of ISKCON. Even if you don't agree you can always ask yourself, can you really control the result in all aspects of your life? Perhaps our answer will sound a bit dicey. We can only try.

—Profiled by Ashutosh 'Skill Hut'

Content

Across the Turning Point

Autumn is a second spring! When every leaf is a flower. In fall even leaves become colourful and give the effect of flowers.

Change is the law of the glorious universe, the great cosmic order. On the earth level, the weathers sustain the health and well-being of humanity and the nature entire. In a household the change is the order of lifestyle, diet, colour of dresses and paints of all variety. It is the... relationship. In vocations, changes of duties and job locations sustain the professional interest avoiding boredom and stresses that affect individual psycho-physiology and human relations with elders and juniors.

This brings as to retirement status, a change from job to joblessness unless one is already assigned a secondment or another official appointment as happens to many an elder professionals. Some secretaries, police commissioners and generals get retired without any indications of such an opportunity. In such a case the retiree becomes a subject of study of his personality factors of stress, attitude towards family, behaviour with associates, all affecting mutual make up affecting the body condition. Even in physical stability marked changes are observed by near and dear ones.

Before proceeding further on the matter, I may mention about all of those retirees who by their very nature of communication, do not have any pangs or negative feelings. They display compassion all the time. Let me recall when a defence officer was superseded believably on political involvement but his associates found no change whatsoever in his performance of the assigned duty, something like the karma yoga of *Geeta*. He soon rose to a high rank and there again was no change towards egotism. And when he retired, he shaved no change in his attitude and the spirit of compassion. He gave of his meagre funds even though he had no source of earnings but pension. He took to teaching of yoga without ego of his status and also without charging any fees. He was invited to several countries abroad where for ten years he was hosted and cared for by students. They knew of his high defence status and were astonished at his *sannyaas* like simplicity. After the decade he took to rural development in his ancestral village where he started a primary school with the help of the state policy. Here too he loved simply shoulder to shoulder with villagers after riding a bullock cart carrying loads like tubewell pump and mango samplings to develop old garden groves.

This example of change without change is rare continuing as he goes his busy chores now mostly as chief editor and author of laudable books at age passing 90 still continuing his yoga-based work-outs. Many a compatriots have found the stage of retirement somewhat difficult to overcome yielding to indoor social charges like card games and alcoholism.

We may see that the different meanings in different context are giving quite negative connotations indicating towards relaxation away from the active life. A businessman, a lawyer or a doctor never feels the pinch of this word. He looks for working life as long as he is keeping in perfect health. The date of retirement for a person in the job is fixed well ahead of the year depends on the policies of the organization. It may be 58 or 60 or 65 as in the case of judges. Do we really need to retire or to have the feeling of retirement? Especially, when thinking about it gives the stress to your mind. Let's see how we spend our life if the work life is 70 years. Some studies were conducted for recognizing the active years of working life and the findings came quite surprising.

We are sleeping for 25 years, we spend 8 years while studying, illness makes us to take rest for 6 years, holidays are enjoyed by us for 7 years, we spend 8 years while commuting, eating takes 4 years of our life which means we have only 12 years of stressful life to work.

If we go by the above study then there should not be any worry about the retirement. Because most of the time we are relaxed. Somebody asked the question to me that I am only talking about working life when stress is there in personal life also. Who says you are not working at home. So where is the question of retirement as long as you are living? Another surprising thing comes that we are only talking about our retirement and do not think about the spouse who is a housewife. Even in the case when the wife is working one hardly feels concerned about her retirement because it is a male-dominated society, a working women shoulders the responsibility of the housewife as well as of her profession. I never appreciated the talks on retirement only in respect of men. Therefore, when we are debating on the issue of retirement let us go for husband and wife both.

A question comes as to whether we really retire or it is just breaking of relationship with the present employer. As a matter of fact, the important factor is our health and physical fitness which makes us to think for retirement. If you ask yourself "Do you really want to retire?" I think the answer will come in most of the cases as negative. Sometimes, the surroundings make you to feel for retirement. The retirement notice 3 months before the date makes you alert for filling up necessary forms, completing formalities to take your terminal benefits, etc. if you are in service.

Feeling the heat

Don't complain about growing old, many people do not have that privilege. Ageing is not lost youth but a new stage or opportunity and strength.

The months...then the days...are counted by you when you are nearing the date of retirement. At times you may feel certain change in the behaviour of people around you. In government service, if you are required to appraise the performance by way of annual confidential reports your status and respect is uplifted by the people who are concerned about it. You also become conscious about your authority of making career of the people at the fag-end of your service. Earlier during the service period, you never noticed certain change of behaviour and level of respect but now it has come as an open secret. The subordinates, who had no guts to ask for good reports, now feel comfortable in taking the liberty of asking this favour, sometime as a matter of right.

The family front seems to be quite well prepared to meet this natural event, specially your spouse. Let me tell you it is only your spouse who will have the real concept of empathy, because she has to live with you for the rest of the life, with constraints or otherwise. I am not trying to make you bias for or against your children but you need to accept the fact that there is a change in their priorities. If your son is married having kids he will feel more concerned about his own family, may be living with you. Well if you have only one son he will be interested only about your terminal benefits or pension so as to feel relaxed that your retirement is not going to give any extra financial burden to him.

You will observe that suddenly you feel concern about the talks of the people and try to find meanings between the lines. If somebody has said, "Oh, you are going to live with your son after retirement", this will become quite offensive because it reflects your dependency on the son. You expect from the people that they still maintain that your son is going to live with you. There is a great difference in the matter of feeling for these two concepts as to whether your son is living with you or you are living with your son. You become quite emotional for certain issues which were not so meaningful earlier.

I do not want to confine my discussion on retirement to the people who are in the job because if, I relate this term with tiredness due to age factor I think at a certain age every human being feels to have relaxation if not physically but mentally. Therefore, this topic of retirement will be discussed in phases when I will come to the planning stage. You may have your business or own consultancy when you feel that I am not going to retire but still as I said, it will be natural at a particular stage of your life when your priority, your interest and hobbies may undergo a change. You may be inclined towards religion or spiritualism, you may feel more concern about your health, and interest towards monitory gains may start losing. These are all indications of your recognizing the existence of the concept of retirement. I feel you must be clear by now that retirement is not just a condition of employment but it is a feeling coming from within. Some people may differ with me citing the example of persons who came into active life after the so-called age of retirement but, if, I go by majority view these cases will be termed as rare ones.

Getting a different identity

The words old, aged, retiree or elderly are some of the jargons which are used for you when you are a retired person. All these words contain an element of despair. I know that no retired person would like to be identified with these titles rather they will tend to refuse to identify themselves as old or aged. It is not uncommon to find many people in the retired category who refuse to even look at themselves in the mirror but you can't help it you need to accept the reality since it is fate accompli. It is law of nature. As we have already discussed old age is the last stage of the life cycle, which starts from birth and its end is death.

A lot of research is being done to categorise the retired people. The following five types of individuals are significant to be known:

1. "Mature" who accepts himself and lives realistically without regret.
2. "Rocking chair" who because of the passivity in the past welcomes a change to be free from responsibilities.
3. "Armour" whose well-developed defences continue to serve in the old age.
4. "Angry" who continues to blame his own weaknesses on others.
5. "Self-hater" who is disappointed with his life and continues to look back in disappointment and

self-resentment.

Retirement is not always disadvantageous. There are certain positive points like freedom from irksome restraints of work and opportunity to do the things for which one had no time earlier. The disadvantage is that unless you have planned you do not have any definite task to perform. The loss of income may be there inspite of taking a new job. Some setbacks in terms of moral and spiritual level in the form of sense of worth and locus of social participation which after retirement diminishe to a great extent. It is quite apparent in social norms that a retired person suffers from identity crises. Recent breakdown of status which was enjoyed by family now they prefer to lead independent life. In most of the cases the children consider elderly people as burden on them. It is painful as our culture shows little indulgence for dependent behaviour. Even the society encourages youth more devaluing the age and experience of elderly people. Somehow, a retired person is considered more dominating and rigid in his attitude.

A retired person gets a new name and identity for respect as senior citizen but let me tell you that this concept of senior citizen may be relevant in Indian scenario only where you get air, railway concession, rebate in income tax, some seats reserved in buses. It is really a matter of reality that you become senior just by virtue of age otherwise during your entire service career you may encounter the bosses who are much younger to you but they are senior. You get a licence to teach others the lessons of etiquettes, morality, discipline and spiritualism.

The word Senior citizen attached with you not only gives certain privilege but also acts as a mark of respect to your age and experience in life. You know that maturity never comes with age but still there is a feeling that you are matured, well experienced though sometime you realize that younger generation is having better perceptions for finding solutions to the problems but still they give credit to your viewpoint and you feel elevated.

Whatever I may say for retirement but still I am not convinced that you ever retire because I feel that it is a matter of mindset. A person may become old even in his 30s and may remain young in his 60s. A lot depends on upbringing, family background, the environment where you were born and brought up. A person of foreign origin may have different concept towards life because his vision and understanding towards life is different from a normal Indian. Recently, I went to Singapore as a speaker and chairperson of an International Summit and my talk was on Managing Stress. I was quite surprised to know when most of the people told me that they do not do exercise, even when they are in their late 30s. They do not feel stress coming out of emotional and psychological stressors. There was no planning in their mind for retirement. I feel that this material on retirement may not be so relevant and useful if, you are planning to settle abroad or you are having your bonding there. Even after explaining all about retirement, I am leaving this introductory chapter with the question "Do we really retire?"

Planning a Second Inning

It's not that some people have will power and some don't. It's that some people are ready to change and others are not.

It is not only career which has to be planned but you must plan for the changes which revolve like a wheel across the axis of life. When you contemplating how to plan your retirement it involves emotional, psychological, financial, health, time, spiritual, reviving hobbies, etc. In some extreme cases even for matrimony, you need planning. I am not joking when I tell you that certain cases have been reported when a man married after the death of his wife to a woman, a widow, who happened to be his girlfriend in his young days. It really came in his life as a fulfilment of his long cherished desire which was lying somewhere dormant in mind. The children of this man were settled abroad and he thought it proper to seek their consent which came quite readily. A person who is financially secure may feel like beginning a new life.

Retirement is no doubt a major landmark in one's life and I feel that organizations too have a moral responsibility to facilitate this transition from one stage of life to another. You have every right to live in dignified manner happily even though you may not be working anymore. It gives you more freedom to take decisions about your personal likes and dislikes.

When I talk about planning for retirement, my idea is for fulfilment of those passions and desires which were left behind, the hobbies which you could not pursue while you were in a profession. Now it is the time to explore hidden talents and fulfil your deepest desire. Take the example of Winston Churchill who attained name and fame after the age of 65 or look at Sardar Patel and Jawaharlal Nehru what they did after 60, Morarji Desai became Prime Minister of India when he was over 80 years of age. Age is never a barrier. You don't become old because of your age, its all in the mind. You are as young as before provided you keep very good health. There are countries in the world like Switzerland, Singapore, Australia, Canada, etc. where care is taken of you in your old age by way of offering social security schemes. But in our country we need to plan our retirement as there is no such security blanket for the elderly. For that matter you must seek help of a financial consultant so that you can invest for the future while you are still working.

Life in phases

Just think that to be 70 years young is sometimes far more cheerful and hopeful than to be 40 years old. Planning for retirement is to be done in different phases like a cycle. Let me start with the first phase which I refer to as the ***Remote Phase*** which begins several years prior to the actual retirement date. Nobody expects to die before reaching retirement age and few expect to keep working till death. Financial security and leisure skills are two important factors which are visualized in the remote phase.

The second phase can be identified as the ***Near Phase*** which occurs just prior to the date of your retirement. Here you begin to perceive that your colleagues are viewing you in a short-term perspective. Involvement in major programmes is discouraged and at times you may be asked to provide training to your replacement. You find yourself busy in the second phase with retirement ceremonies, farewell, etc.

Now, comes the ***Honeymoon Phase,*** which is the third phase of the cycle because after retirement you get the freedom to live out your dreams and fantasies, your finances will permit you to travel, meet old friends, spend time with your grandchildren and so on, and if somebody asks you how life is now after retirement and your answer would probably be "why I have never been so busy". An idea comes to my mind for this phase presume your gratuity is only one lac instead of 3.5 lac because you have planned a holiday package to different countries alongwith your spouse. Don't disclose this plan of spending 2.5 lacs on a holiday package to your wife or else it will never materialize, as she will be against and will probably say, "Have you gone mad burning so much money at 60? Return the tickets at once! I am not going." Well, I shall prepare you to face this situation well in advance. Tell your wife that these tickets are not refundable. A little piece of advice - have the passport of your wife made in first phase, i.e. in the Remote Phase and rest assured you will have a gala second honeymoon in different countries of the world and will have an experience you will cherish till the end of your life. Now your gratuity is going to be 10 lacs so you can have better deals.

Not everyone goes through the fourth phase of the retirement cycle. It is a stage when life finally slows down. The honeymoon is over and a certain amount of dissatisfaction sets in life. It becomes boring; those who have not developed a variety of skills in preparing for retirement are likely to experience this stage more severely. It may be particularly difficult if one has moved to a different community after retirement.

Now comes the fifth phase of the cycle, which may be termed as the ***Reorientation Phase*** where one may attempt to structure a lifestyle that can run for many years. It comes by way of exploring new opportunities and making realistic choices in the light of personal interest and skills.

Now we come to the sixth phase of the cycle which is known as the ***Stability Phase***, when a person develops a philosophy and a pattern of decision-making resulting in a reasonably busy, predictable and satisfying life. In this phase one is able to cope and adapt to declines in physical capability that comes with advancing age. He or she feels self-sufficient.

Lastly, we come to the seventh phase of the cycle, the ***Termination Phase***. One may, of course, die suddenly while experiencing any of the preceding sixth phase of the retirement cycle. If life continues, one could enter the Termination Phase. A few unlucky land up to this stage because of non-planning and for being dependent on others, which may lose the dignity associated with the role of retirement. Please for God's sake do not disclose your Will to your children lest you always remain a giver rather than a taker.

Learn from the life of others

You might have experienced failures in life or undergone certain crisis demotivating you for beginning a second inning. Some people feel depressed because of poor family background and due to financial inconveniences. But remember every dark cloud has a silver lining. We can learn from the history of successful persons in the world who have risen high inspite of failures in life.

Nothing succeeds like success

The name of *Abraham Lincoln*, the US president, comes first for getting encouragement in life from failures. It may be recalled that *Abraham Lincoln* was the son of a poor farmer who lost his job in the beginning of the career, got defeated for legislature, started business but failed. His wife died of a fatal disease and he experienced nervous breakdown. He could not win the election for a speaker even failed to get the nomination from the political party. Once he applied for the post of Land Officer but he was not selected. *Abraham Lincoln* contested for senate and also for vice-president but lost the elections. All these failures never demotivated him and after two years of losing the elections he was elected as president of America.

Never lose the hope

There is a long list of successful people who started with the humble beginning like *Albert Einstein,* the world famous scientist, who was an ordinary clerk. *Mr. M.S. Oberoi,* one of the biggest Hotel Chain owners, was a simple clerk.

If you have any physical disability or some medical problem, don't lose heart. Take inspiration from the people who suffered a lot, but still perform in excellent manner. *Franklin. D. Roosevelt* was sick, with both legs paralysed, but he became president of America. The greatest Greek writer *Homer* was blind. Again the renowned writer *Helen Keller* was not only blind but deaf and dumb also.

The physical disability should not come in your way if you have the talent and courage to pursue a career. The renowned music composer *Beethoven* was deaf. The well known Greek orator *Demosthenes* was nervous stammerer.

Why to talk about foreigners only, in our country *Sharat Kumar Dixit,* the renowned surgeon, performed 45000 surgeries free of cost in spite of suffering with two heart attacks; crippled in lower side of the body with removed vocal cords. The famous swimmer *C.N. Janaki* was suffering with polio of both legs.

You may not be highly educated to begin the second inning but still the ray of hope is there. Think about *Thomas Edison,* who was only a matriculate but became a greatest inventor. The prime minister of Israel, *Goldameir,* was an average school teacher.

Some people say that they do not have money to start business. It is just an excuse because *Topiwala,* a matriculate, made his name for selling five crore worth of *Shingar Bindi* per year though he started business with initial investment of Rs. 100 only.

Let us appreciate that the deficiencies never come in our way when we have the ambition and dreams to rise up in life. President *A.P.J Abdul Kalam* came from a very poor family. Even the largest seller of Nirma washing powder, *K.K. Patel,* was the son of an ordinary farmer who had the turnover of Rs. 1200 crores per year.

Words have no meanings

You may experience in day-to-day life that words have no meaning but we give meanings to the words. At times the meaning of the same word changes from person to person depending upon the mutual wavelength and perception. It is in our hands to give positive or negative meaning to the same word. Look at GODISNOWHERE which can be understood as GOD IS NO WHERE if you want to have negative feeling. Now when you see the same alphabets in positive sense it will be read as GOD IS NOW HERE.

It is the beginning of the second inning of your career. So believe in word "GOD" to have the meanings. G–To generate enthusiasm, O – To operate to your potential and D–To destroy negative attitude.

The change can start with yourself and can begin only within. Don't have passive attitude. Instead of blaming darkness, light a candle if you can. Stop blaming; instead take action.

Look for Emotional Stability

It is the sadness of growing older that will lose our ardent appreciation of what is new and different and difficult.

Today, Lt. General Subroto Banerjee is a young man at the age of 85, who retired from the armed forces decades ago, that too a premature retirement since due to political reasons he could not become the army chief. For General Banerjee the retirement age was 58 but he had to say goodbye to army when he was 56 only. Let's go down the memory lane to get to know General Subroto Banerjee better.

The childhood of Subroto Banerjee was the golden period of his life for he was born as the son of a Rai Bahadur Shantano Banerjee, an ICS Officer, during the British regime. He had all the comforts and luxuries that a young boy could want, study in a good school, living in huge bungalow with lots of servants, travelling in a Chevrolet car with a handsome pocket money. Subroto turned out to be brilliant student with hobbies like playing piano, singing, swimming, mountaineering. Subroto excelled in studies and sports and earned a name for his school. Though he was selected for Engineering in Thomson College of Engineering, Roorkee, he yearned to join the Army and was an excellent marksman. He dropped the idea of joining engineering and instead joined the Army. He received most of his training in the UK with the Royal Armed Forces.

Subroto Banerjee was fond of going to the club, dancing, drinking and was a member of the Gymkhana Club of Delhi; he was a good tennis and polo player too. The polo club saw him as an excellent player. He fell in love with a girl from the royal family of Rajasthan. She coming from the royal family had different tastes but was a god-fearing lady. Subroto made a great success of this inter-caste marriage though there was a lot of cultural difference. He fought in wars and got a number of medallions for his gallantry. He was blessed with a son and a daughter and he admitted them in Jesuit School in Punchgani. Subsequently they studied in UK. After retirement from ICS, Shantano Banerjee lived a lonely life with his wife at a hill station because Subroto could not serve his parents in their old age mainly because his wife was not willing. She never missed her children who used to come only during the summer holidays. Well, days then years passed. There was so much of turmoil in the career graph of Subroto. But he never compromised with honesty and his values. He lost his promotion to his junior who became the Chief of the Army. His son got into a prestigious engineering college of the country and soon after fulfilling the qualification, one of his friends who was the High Commissioner in the UK invited him to do MBA. Later on his son moved to the USA to join a multinational company as a software engineer. Subroto was a writer and poet but he kept his sentiments to himself because his life partner was of a totally different nature. She preferred to live life each day as it came, attending parties or hosting parties. His parents suffered a lot living alone in their old age.

Subroto visited them once a year. Most of the communication was through letters, that too, when there was some problem. Financially Shantano Banarjee never faced any problem because being a senior bureaucrat of British empire he got a handsome pension and the villa in which he lived on the hill station was his own. Subroto Banarjee felt guilty and often drank alone, listened to music with dim lights. He was eager to serve his parents but somehow he could not convince his wife.

The emotional and psychological stress made Subroto to write poems and to travel abroad in search of peace, which he got in spirituality. He became a kind of *Swami* visiting countries giving the message of peace and teaching yoga. His wife did not approve his lifestyle. She never accompanied him on his spiritual missions. After taking premature retirement at the age of 56, Subroto Banarjee was offered many a lucrative positions because of his high level contacts. Multinational companies those days with no Indian participation offered him the position of director on their board. But Subroto declined them and preferred to live life on his own terms. Finance was never a problem as he had built a beautiful bungalow in Bombay facing the sea. This bungalow became as a mark of financial stability after his retirement because the rent coming from the bungalow was 10 times his pension. His son came back from abroad and joined a multinational company in India. He married a beautiful girl belonging to a different community. She was a beautiful girl because the love marriage was the result of her winning a beauty contest. The same thing happened with the daughter. Subroto received a number of proposals from IAS officers for his daughter but somehow they never materialised. He failed to understand his daughter. Both Subroto and his wife were unaware that their daughter was having an affair with a boy whose only qualification was good dancing skills, boozing habits and handsome looks. She insisted to marrying him and eventually Subroto gave in and also got him a job in a good multinational company for the sake of his daughter.

Subroto's parents hankered for their grandchildren which was not destined. Then they lost their lives in a tragic accident. Subroto and his wife could not be informed about the death in time and by the time they reached the funeral it was over.

Subroto never realised how 15 years passed after retirement while visiting different countries. His wife was comfortable leading a lavish life on the rental income of the bungalow in Bombay. Most of her time was spent partying or drinking, she proved to be a good party person with the capacity of drinking one bottle scotch a day. Quite surprisingly these bad habits never affected her health. All along his married life, Subroto could not have the proper matching with the wife at the emotional or physical level. There was a great distance between them. One can say there was no sharing of feelings, it was just a relationship of husband and wife living under the same roof but as strangers. Subroto enjoyed outside respect by virtue of his rank of Lt. General, a huge friend's circle and recognition for his books and teachings given in different countries.

Subroto's son eventually resigned from the multinational company and started his own business. He sent his children abroad to study and it was a different world for him. The same happened with the daughter, she was living far away in Calcutta. The communication with the parents was only over telephone and that too on a need basis or just to enquire the welfare at long intervals of time. Later Subroto's wife when in her 80s suffered with illnesses which was the result of bad habits. She was hospitalised and finally, in spite of best efforts, could not be saved. It gave a shock to Subroto, which reflects in some poems written by him. The children took this event in a natural manner with the satisfaction that their mother had died at the right age. Subroto was left alone at the mercy of servants and doctors. His money was being enjoyed by the servants and drivers. He had no energy to maintain an account of his earnings and expenses. Money was in abundance because of the high rent he received. It was to the tune of lacs of rupees per month coming in the form of cash and bank transfers.

Lt. General Subroto Banerjee, now in his 80s, looks at tidal waves of the Arabian Sea from the terrace of his bungalow at the Worli Sea face in Bombay and calculates the entire life especially the retired life. Where had he gone wrong? What was the reason for his emotional and psychological suffering? Why money could not give him pleasure? Why could he not have love and affection from his children? What made so much distance in his relationships? Why friends seem to be more important today? Lt. General Subroto Banerjee thinks and thinks alone, going down the memory lane. He feels, he should have planned for emotional stability. Subroto also realises that what he did to his parents, the same was happening with him. Why was he regretting. Is it too late now, at the fag end of his life?

Let's debate to recognise the importance and requirement of planning for psychological and emotional stability at the time of retiring.

When I think of the answers to the above story, the

importance of emotional and psychological planning seems primary because with old age comes mood swings, depression, loss of memory, restlessness, anger, anxiety and suicidal thoughts. Therefore, you have to understand these emotional and psychological factors which cause enormous stress. Before I go for any other planning, I feel it is most important to give due weightage to the emotional and psychological aspects first. You may not agree with the symptoms but let me tell you that your behaviour will indicate and justify the need for planning in this area of your mental and physical state. People may observe certain behavioural changes in you which may vary from person to person. It could be gnashing teeth, a wrinkling forehead, foot tapping, nail biting, hair pulling, increased smoking, compulsive dieting and pacing about.

However, you cannot go for this emotional planning unless you have realization about the above behavioural and emotional factors. I would like to reiterate that these symptoms can not be generalised. Some people may feel them some may not, but still when it comes to the question of planning in a proactive manner I would like to advocate it for everybody. Just think that you are a senior citizen when you are old and it is expected that after crossing the age of 60 you have your grandchildren and your own children who are now in their middle age. With the passage of time one becomes old. There is no effort on your part in the ageing process, it is natural. After crossing 40 years you suffer with a feeling of becoming old. Each year after 40 makes you to feel as if something has been snatched from your body. You no longer enjoy your birthdays as you did earlier. You start looking back and this period of transition between the age of 40 and 60 passes in the blink of eyes.

Expectations versus reality

At 60 your stress level is high and apart from that you suffer from various things. You start expecting too much from your spouse and children. You are sensitive to smallest of things. It always comes to your mind that they were so caring. The grandchildren when they were born were given in your hands. You remember their love for you. They were always in your lap as if they could not live without you. You remember the days when your children used to seek your advice and your decisions were implemented. You know that the career of your children was planned by you. They always acted on your advice. Now they have stopped consulting you, your grandchildren are spending less time with you, you may be suffering with multiple diseases requiring constant visits to doctors, you worry about the expenditure especially on you, you are hesitant in asking for food of your choice, at times you feel like going out to see a movie or a play but you prefer to wait when your children will take you. You lose interest in clothes and now it is religion which becomes dearer to you. You feel like going to religious places and worship regularly. Suddenly you find that there is a change in the thinking process of three generations before you, i.e. you, your children and your grandchildren. You accept it as generation gap.

Stress is not a new thing. You have faced enough of it in your life. You know about the remedies too but now things are different. You feel a sense of insecurity and dependence. You look for love and affection as if it is not coming automatically from near and dear ones. You feel a lack of belongingness. You start losing self-esteem. These are weak moments during old age which are natural and you are unaware about the factors responsible for it. When you go to a party with your children your expectations become high and you wish that everybody will receive you with a full heart. You anticipate a gesture on their face. You look for respect and their attention towards you. You fear of not getting all these things. You feel frustrated and depressed for not getting the expected and desired behaviour of the people and you are unable to understand the change in behaviour of the people who matters to you. When you were in service you suffered with the trauma of retirement. After retirement your financial position becomes weak. You feel dependent on others and often envy the people of your age who are running their business or consultancy. You call up your grandchildren and at times compel them to spend time with you, even when you know that there is reluctance on their part. You feel sorry for no rhyme or reason and when you are not able to confront your children you tend to blame your spouse and start arguments to have a win or lose situation without realising she too is getting on in years.

The above instances reflect the physical and emotional breakdown you are suffering from. There is nothing abnormal in these realities and expectations. These are life situations. When I am talking about the remedies to come out of the above instances, it is very clear that you know it. You need to have self-realisation. Go down the memory lane. Try to remember the days how you behaved with your parents and grandparents when you were young. For people who were fortunate to have their grandparents with them, remember the time you spent with them. Now see what is coming out of the introspection. I am sure you've got an answer for your miseries. Now analyze each situation which made you tensed because of their behaviour. Step into the shoes of others so as to know where the shoe pinches. You must understand that times are changing. There is a change in the value system. A great amount of modernization has taken place and now there are different social norms. Be practical. Live and let others live. You had earned your bread and eaten it well. Now there is time for your children and grandchildren to live their life. Don't give unnecessary and unwanted advice. Don't interfere especially when your indulgence and advice is not solicited. Pretend to be ignorant for things when you were not involved. Respect your position. Feel proud of your deeds.

I know that my advice sounds very idealistic and you are finding it impractical to follow. But believe me there is no other way to live a stress-free life with joy except by adopting a positive outlook. Think positive, do positive and look positive. Don't give room for negative thoughts. You can't afford to neglect your health, which is withering away each passing day. I need to repeat "health is wealth", especially at old age these words have greater meaning. You will not care for it unless you see your colleagues in the same age group passing days bed-ridden, suffering from incurable diseases. Keep your sex life live as long as you can with the co-operation of your partner. Religion is important to preach and practice. It is a matter of faith. You may be a person who doesn't believe in God but at least have an impression in your mind that there is some supernatural power controlling the entire universe.

You must do breathing exercise, breathe rhythmically, hold your breath and release it slowly. Some people have the notion that holding your breath for sustainable time increases life span. Well, I can't say whether it is true or false but it is good to have proper control of your breath. Yoga should be a way of life for you. Consult your doctor before you go for yogic exercises. Relaxation is also important because you get physically exhausted easily.

As I have mentioned earlier, you must have least expectations. Don't keep things in your heart about the way people treat you, try to adopt the policy of feel and forget. You have to avoid *"hurry, worry and curry"* come what may. Anxiety would become poison for you. You must remember always that you cannot afford to be anxious now for anything whatever it may be. You will feel comfortable both emotionally and psychologically if you live each day as it comes. Always bear in mind that whatever you meet in life is fixed but how you meet it is not fixed. Therefore, be happy with whatever you have rather than cry for what you don't have.

Be aware of imported love of your children

Young men's minds are always changeable, but when an old man is concerned in a matter, he looks both before and after. Let us see what the following story teaches us.

Gayatri Devi and her husband were living a happy retired life in Delhi with regular source of income by way of husband's pension and rental of the first floor of their house as the only regular income. Her son was well settled in London and daughter was in United States. Both children were happy with their family. They visited India atleast once in two years. Neither son nor daughter invited the old couple to live with them in the UK or the USA. After three years of marriage, their son started calling up Gayatri Devi frequently to her surprise because in the past there was hardly any communication from her son. She had no expectation from her daughter-in-law.

One fine morning, Gayatri Devi got a pleasant surprise when she found her son at her doorstep. Her husband was also surprised to see their son after such a long time. It was a matter of great joy when they learnt that very soon they were going to become grandparents. The son disclosed his purpose of coming. It was to take Gayatri Devi to London with the excuse that daughter-in-law was feeling lonely and was missing her. Initially, Gayatri Devi was reluctant to leave her husband alone since there was no offer for the husband to go along with her, but she could not muster up her courage to suggest to take her husband along with them. Her husband supported the idea and agreed to send her.

Gayatri Devi could not adjust to the new environment and felt lonely. Since nobody was there, she took full care of the household work. She missed her husband, but the joy of becoming the grandmother kept her going. The daughter-in-law was busy in her work and she hardly had even one hour with her son to talk in the whole day and night. The day Gayatri Devi was blessed with a grandson, it was the first occasion when she got the opportunity to have a long conversation with her husband sharing her happiness with him. Quite willingly she took the entire responsibility of the infant. The daughter-in-law was obliviously very happy.

After a year of caring her grandson, one day she came to through their neighbours at India know that her husband was unwell. Gayatri Devi became impatient to go back to India, however, her daughter-in-law did not allow her to be back. Her daughter-in-law consoled that things would be alright. She promised to employ an attendant to look after her father-in-law. But Gayatri Devi did not give in and she flew back to India. Only after meeting her husband she realized that his sickness was due to loneliness.

Gayatri Devi was feeling quite relaxed with her husband though sometimes she was having a desire that her husband should visit their son to see the grandchild, so that he may also enjoy the company of their grandson. The repeated telephone calls from her son and daughter-in-law from London made her to believe that they love her immensely. It gave her the feeling as if they all were missing her. She could not say a single word when her son did not show any interest in taking the father along. They were repeatedly requesting her to come for the sake of her grandson. Gayatri Devi ultimately went to England and two years passed like that when time came for grandson to go to school. She came back to India when her husband was seriously ill and subsequently he died. It was a turning point in her life because now, there were no calls or requests from her son or daughter-in-law to come to England.

What do we learn from this story? I am addressing this issue to the retired people both male and female. Was it true love and affection of the children or were they looking for a caretaker for the children? Please pardon me if I say a housemaid? Because whether it is USA or UK you cannot afford to keep a housemaid. It may cost your entire salary in real terms. I am not casting any aspersion on the natural love and affection for a grandmother by her grandson or for a son by his mother but in reality the love vanishes once they don't require a caretaker like in the case mentioned above. I wish no retired person should suffer emotional blackmail due to this imported love.

There are exceptions of course when a son calls either parents to the UK and USA or wherever they are staying so that they may enjoy the company of the grandchildren and the son.

Born abroad brought up in India

Much different from the above instance of 'imported' love in USA and UK the latest trend is to have the children born in India and raised by the grandparents. It serves dual purpose. First heavy saving on medical expenditure for delivery of the child abroad and natal care. As compared to India the cost of having a child abroad is exorbitant. Thanks to various international schools in India which provide excellent education at a marginal cost as compared to what it costs abroad. Again, if your son or daughter is settled abroad it is a good plan to have the child born in India and also brought up to primary level or secondary level then migrate later for higher education to settle abroad. The parents if they have citizenship of other countries it is not a problem for the grandson or daughter to settle.

One of my friends from the US told me that hiring a babysitter in the US is expensive and non-personal. No amount of dollars can provide the kind of personal care which they get from their relatives in India. To give a touch of reality and genuineness to my saying let me rely on a study conducted in Andhra Pradesh for over 1000 such children who are **US citizen by birth but born and brought up in India**. The Telugu Association of North America (TANA), the largest body of American Telugus, has confirmed that there could be over 5000 such children residing in Andhra Pradesh. In Hyderabad itself, a total of 1500 US citizens are registered with police out of which 75% are children below 4 years. US passport apart they hold Persons of Indian Origin (PIO) cards.

Look at the sentimental part of it. You miss your children who are settled abroad but you feel happy that atleast the grandchildren are with you. At the same time, your son or daughter would feel happy that their children are being cared by the grandparent. Sometime in-laws also take pride in bringing up their grandchildren. Your children would argue that upbringing in India inculcate the deep-rooted Indian values and provide emotional mooring in the child so that he or she can face the realities of life in the USA or the UK. It is really a win-win situation for your children who are foreign citizens. But, the irony is that when your grandchild after completing the primary education is taken back by their parents you suffer from the emptyness syndrome. I have met such retired people and interacted with them. It is really difficult for them to adjust to the situation when their grandchild leaves them. They miss the child so much — his room, his toys, his belongings, his talks and memories of playing games together. All these fond memories bring tears in their eyes.

I cannot generalise the above instances to say that they are common happenings but in majority of the cases one needs to be careful that he is not being blackmailed by superficial imported love. Love needs to be natural, spontaneous and permanent. It cannot be artificial and shortlived. Please do not allow your children encash it. Discuss the things openly with pros and cons on the ground reality of the situation. If you are satisfied that this shortlived love can give you happiness go ahead enjoy it without keeping any room for expectations.

Matrimony—A Thought Away

It is a mistake to regard age as a downhill grade towards dissolution. The reverse is true. As one grows older, one climbs with surprising strides.

You must be surprised to find this title in this book, but in some rare cases it becomes necessary during the lifetime, if not, at the time of retirement. There are few unfortunate one's who never had a happy, contented married life.

Professor Mukesh Bhardwaj is the faculty of an internationally reputed Management School. His books brought out by reputed publishers are considered the best reference books on the subjects across the world. He teaches at the Indian Institute of Management, Ahmedabad. He has no dearth of money. His lectures abroad fetch him US$1000 per hour. Mostly he remains on tour on invitations to different parts of the country and abroad.

Today, Professor Mukesh Bhardwaj is 60 and about to retire. For his students and colleagues he is the icon of success; the royalty for his books is in lacs. He is a man paying income tax in lacs but ask him if he is happy? It is a big question! Because the professor in him will debate on the definition of happiness. Let's analyse what all Professor Bhardwaj has lost and gained in his life. A brilliant student, born in a rich business family of Delhi, he set records right from schooling to graduation from the prestigious St. Stephen College of Delhi and then moved abroad, did his Master's from Harvard University and then Doctorate from the University of California, Los Angeles. Somehow he never wanted to settle abroad, may be because of Divya, the love of his life. An intelligent beautiful girl Divya was an MBA and a PhD from Delhi University, teaching Management. They were childhood sweethearts. They got married and were blessed with a daughter and then a son. They were living a very happy married life, maintaining good relations with friends and associates, writing was a passion for Divya too.

One fine morning Prof. Bhardwaj decided to take a weekend holiday to Mussoorie. It was planned after dinner day earlier. Divya suggested to start early in the morning in their new Toyota Corrola so as to reach Mussoorie early. Divya ensured that the daughter is ready by 5O' clock and but the small son while asleep was taken in her lap. It was a smooth drive due to dividers on the road. However on the way, all of a sudden near Meerut Prof. Bhardwaj saw a truck driver approaching from the opposite direction on the same road. The truck driver was on the wrong lane. Prof. Bhardwaj gave the dipper with the anticipation that truck driver will take care by giving him side. He was finding it difficult to control the speed which was 120 km per hour and the result was head-on collision. Next morning Prof. Bhardwaj found himself in a nursing home by that time he lost his world. He lost his wife Divya and son. And his daughter was struggling for life. Two months of leave could not heal his trauma. Many a times Prof. Bhardwaj thought to commit suicide, but the thought of his daughter gave him courage to live. The relatives and parents forced him to marry again to a qualified divorced PhD scholar who was teaching in Delhi University. Prof. Bhardwaj was in his late 40s at that time. Marriage for him at this juncture was a compromise for his daughter, but his second wife had so many dreams for a new married life. The arguments started from the beginning since Prof. Bhardwaj could not forget Divya, though the daughter was left with the grandparents.

The next five years in the life of Prof. Bhardwaj were of great turmoil. He suffered mental agony and torture due to strained relationship with his second wife. The matter did not end there; since there were police complaints from the side of his wife with false allegations of dowry and what not. Finally with the help of some advocate friends Prof. Mukesh Bhardwaj got a mutual divorce and paid Rs. 50 lacs as settlement amount to second wife. Meanwhile, his daughter was growing up and she got into Vellore Institute of Technology for the course of Computer Engineering.

The loneliness and remembrance of the past years spent with Divya were the only pass time for Prof. Bhardwaj. Though he felt young mentally and now this time he wanted to enjoy his life. He entered into an affair with Priya, a Professor at Indian Institute of Management, Ahmedabad where he joined as Dean. He was enjoying a live-in relationship but he never knew the hidden agenda in the mind of Prof. Priya, who was too close to him now. The age gap between them was more than 10 years but still Priya compelled Prof. Bhardwaj to marry her. In the eyes of society it was not a desirable move on the part of Prof. Bhardwaj but somehow though nearing the age of 60, he agreed to marry her.

Money had never been an issue. Suddenly, against medical advice Priya thought of having a child for which

Prof. Bhardwaj was not willing. It was a beginning of torture again. The matter was settled when doctors finally declared that Priya cannot conceive due to her age factor. Now it was a stage of blaming from the side of Priya and she started finding excuses to harass Prof. Bhardwaj. Though, he had no patience to decide the remedial action to have peace so he devoted most of his time in writings and going for research in the library. Now six months are left for him to retire however he can still be there on contract basis but Prof. Mukesh Bhardwaj was convinced that he needed to retire owning to his failing health.

Looking into the life of Prof. Mukesh Bhardwaj especially from the matrimonial point of view gives rise to questions. How many times can a person marry, on valid grounds of death of the spouse or a divorce? One has to ensure in what way a second or third marriage can be planned for securing a happy retired life because in the old age you become more dependent on your spouse. Who will listen to you? Your children will keep on changing priorities and when you retire somehow your number in their priority list will go inch below. We have talked a lot about this aspect in emotional planning; there is no doubt that a retired person cannot have happiness and peace of mind without the company of his or her spouse. Death of your spouse is not in your hands though, divorce is. But marriage after marriage, is it the solution? How can one ensure that the partner will be suitable in a subsequent attempt? Take it granted that you cannot forget the good memories of the past, your first honeymoon and the children from your first spouse. The life span and the marriages of Prof. Mukesh Bhardwaj need to be analysed as food for thought to learn.

Entertaining reality

In Switzerland normally children move out of their home after school to be independent. There is social security scheme which takes care of all your needs in the old age. Nobody is rich or poor there. You cannot acquire property to become rich so at one level a shopkeeper and a tram driver both have the same standard of living. Old people do not feel so much sentimentally attached with their children. They may meet only on weekends or if, there is any family function, etc.

Many of you must have seen in movies where a man marries in old age with his old girl friend but my interaction with people in Zurich, Switzerland gave me the new experience of witnessing certain interesting events. I feel it is relevant to discuss a true story in the context of matrimonial planning after retirement. One evening I was discussing late night with Indian community and we were making lot of noise by way of talking and singing songs when suddenly one boy kicked at our door and requested us to lower our voice since elderly couple were living on the ground floor.

On the face of above situation, I gave an idea to students to invite the couple for a cup of coffee, because it was still not bed time. My suggestion made all of us to go downstairs instead of troubling the old couple to come up. We were welcomed. While interacting with the couple, I was surprised to know that they were having their honeymoon. I was anxious to know the full facts. The old man was feeling so lively and happy when he told me that they had married just 10 days before and the lady happened to be his girlfriend when he was 25 and she was 20. They were now in their seventies. To cut a long story short the old man told me that somehow he could not marry her earlier and it remained a painful affair with so many untold sentiments. They got married at different places, got their life partners lived happily with children settled in the US. Now, just a fortnight back after a long gap of over 40 years, they happened to meet and could recognize each other instantly. The lady had just lost her husband and was now widow and the old man also lost his wife recently. It was an occasion of reviving old feelings. Age was not a stumbling block, the old forgotten love and the sentiments embedded in the remote corner of heart suddenly surfaced. After the party the old man rang up the lady and talked at length. It took no time in getting the consent of children from both sides and they went to the church to get married.

Later, I thought what a good idea of having matrimonial planning specially for the people who lost their love in young age. We cannot generalize these situations because such instances are rare but I felt happy to know that old man feels so happy and now busy telling me that he has no time because he has lot of things he wants to tell his new wife which he could not tell in the young age during courtship. They are madly in love feeling on top of the world. When I narrated this incident to my Indian friends their remarks were quite surprising. Instead of feeling happy they felt that it was wrong because both of them should have been mourning for their lost spouses. According to them, it was ridiculous because according to Indian tradition they should have been "devoting time in garlanding the big portraits of the departed soul, and praying for the peace."

Somehow, I am not here to buy this argument of mourning and spending the life with tears. It is just a matter of chance that both lost their spouses. This situation was not created, it happened unfortunately. Then why one should not look for peace and happiness after retirement if this kind of matrimony is possible. Just think about it.

Remaining young at heart

The concept of live-in relationship is slowly becoming common in our country also where more and more young couples are living together without entering into wedlock. Here, I am not going to suggest as to what you should do because all these options may or may not come in your life.

Age is not a bar for a marriage. In the western countries love after 50 is not an uncommon phenomenon. Celebrities marry with girls half their age. There are instances in history where Nobel laureates, heads of states and eminent artists whose heart became young seeking love in old age. For instance, Nelson Mandela, Nicolas Sarkozi of France, Salman Rushdie, Vladimir Putin of Russia. Look at the matrimonial life of these great personalities. Nelson Mandela married Evlinson in 1944. After 13 years the marriage ended in divorce and Mandela married Winni but this marriage also did not last and he divorced her in 1996. Nelson Mandela became young at the age of 80 when he married a third time with Greca Machela. Another interesting man whose reference is necessary in this context is Salman Rushdie. His first marriage was in 1976 with Clarisa Luward and second marriage in 1988 with novelist Marianne Vigginis and the third marriage in 1997 with Elizabeth and the last marriage was with Padma Laxmi which has also broken up.

In India the name of Pandit Ravi Shankar comes foremost in the mind followed by many film personalities who had numerous liaisons in their late 50s and 60s. Today, their numbers are so high that it is pointless to name them. Everyday we read in the newspaper about a new love story. It is hard to believe that young girls in their 20s fall in love with a man nearing in 50s. These love affairs are not only talked about but accepted in the society. However, don't be influenced by these. Take it just as general knowledge because for adding your name in the list you need to be a great celebrity or a millionaire or a person of high status. Middle class men please stay away in old age from such liaisons because if you venture into it you will be outcasted by the society and your children will disown you. Your entire reputation will be at stake.

No upper age for marriage

World over there is no bar to marry in old age. Here are some interesting facts of lower age limits for marriages in different countries:

India	:	21 years for men and 18 for women
USA	:	16 years for men and women with the consent of parents
Pakistan	:	18 years for men and 16 years for women

In the countries like South Africa a girl can marry even at the tender age of 12 years. Saudi Arabia is one step ahead to justify the marriage of 9 years old girl.

See with all lower age limits there is no upper age for marriage. My idea of giving these details is not to encourage the second marriage, but just to say that upper age is not there anywhere in the world for marriage. It is for man and woman both. It is a matter of personal choice and liking which depends on the circumstances of individual concerned. No one can generalise the situation. Therefore one should take independent decision for his own satisfaction to look for happiness.

Money—The Strongest Support

For man, autumn is a time of harvest, of gathering together
For nature, it is a time of sowing, of scattering abroad

Rajiv Mehta is now 62 years old and looking for a job desperately. He has no choice for profession and is willing to work on any terms or conditions to meet the basic requirements of food and shelter. You may be thinking that I am talking about an illiterate poor man. No it is not so. Let's find out what exactly happened with Rajiv Mehta.

Rajiv Mehta was a bright student in school and had secured very high marks in his secondary exams. He was the eldest son of a bureaucrat, a pampered child right from the beginning. One can say that he was born with the proverbial silver spoon in his mouth. We are talking of the times when there were limited numbers of engineering colleges in the country. He got into a prestigious engineering college and completed his graduation. He was fortunate to get a job in an organisation which later became Public Sector Company. It was a British company earlier; therefore, Rajiv Mehta enjoyed the British legacy by way of big bungalows, servants, club membership, playing golf and billiards. It was a very satisfactory happy life with good money as well as comforts and status. After marriage Rajiv was blessed with a son a and daughter. He spent all his earnings for affording the best convent education for his two children. He maintained the bungalow in an excellent manner and was very particular about the antiques in his drawing room or the unique furniture. He was also very fond of dogs and kept several of them.

A turning point came in his life when he was 53. His son could not succeed in any competitive exams and wanted to join a private engineering college. There was a requirement of donation of Rs.8 lac plus an expenditure of Rs.5000 per month apart from the fees amounted Rs.2 lac per year. Rajiv had never believed in saving money except for the compulsory savings in provident fund account. Now, all of a sudden this requirement of nearly 14 lac came as a rude shock for which he was not prepared. You may say it was love for his son or pressure from his wife that he opted for voluntary retirement to get a lump sum amount of about 20 lac rupees as golden handshake. It was an unplanned move, just to meet the immediate requirement for his son's career. Though, there were many options before his son to do graduation and study further but he was adamant to join the private engineering college, thinking that it was the duty of his father to provide the best education to the children.

After taking premature retirement, Rajiv got employment with a marketing company in the private sector on the strength of his background and experience of international marketing, visiting different countries organising trade fairs, etc. Rupees15 lac went for his son's education and somehow he was wise enough to deposit 5 lac with the post office for a fixed deposit. Another big task was left behind of marrying off his daughter. Rajiv had never planned his daughter's marriage. He had never thought of saving money for this planned expenditure. The post office fixed deposit of Rs.5 lac was a meager amount for marriage. Fortunately, Rajiv's mother was still alive, though he had lost his father, but mother was living with his brother. How to generate money for his daughter's marriage? This was a big question before Rajiv. His wife suggested selling the ancestor's jewellery and also to take jewellery from his mother. Being the eldest son, Rajiv was lucky to have inherited a good amount of jewellery which was given to him right from his childhood to marriage and onwards. It was pure gold which fetched very handsome amount in the gold market. Rajiv could got Rs.15 lac by way of selling the jewellery and celebrated his daughter's marriage in a lavish manner and saved rest of the 2 lac.

Rajiv inherited a legacy of honesty and maintaining his value system based on sincerity and devotion to work. He never compromised with his values and ethics. While working in a private sector somehow for 5-6 years he could afford to maintain his value system, since the prevailing unethical practices started giving bad air to Rajiv and he felt suffocated due to pollution of corruption. It was difficult to get the fresh air of honesty in private sector. Rajiv suffered great tragedy when his son met with an accident and required major surgery and hospitalization for a year for an estimated expenditure of Rs.10 lac. There was no source from where he could take loan. Therefore, he encashed the post office's FDRs and the money from selling his ancestral jewellery at the time of daughter's marriage. He also sold out the entire household items including the expensive antiques, furniture and electronic gadgets and was left penniless, but fortunately his son got well. He was now desperate, ready to move anywhere for work. Some of his contacts helped him get a consultancy job with the state government in Gujarat where he got accommodation with comfortable salary to meet two ends.

The government sector was also bound by rules and regulations where they cannot engage a consultant over 62 years of age. Rajiv was again on the crossroads looking for a job after completion of his tenure with the government. Somehow his bureaucratic contacts worked and he got a job with a very big private sector company. Because of his honesty, straightforwardness and sincerity he exposed a scandal harming the organisation for crores. The people involved in the corrupt practices could not tolerate the existence of Rajiv in the organisation and the chief executive against his wishes, was compelled to remove him from the organisation.

Rajiv Mehta was again standing on the threshold in a dilemma and was compelled to live with his son at Hyderabad who is working for a multinational company on a package of 26 lacs per year. It is not known whether his son and daughter-in-law are happy to keep him and his wife. But one thing is certain, i.e. self-ego of Rajiv on the strength of his background which is not allowing him to live with his son.

Today, Rajiv Mehta is a man of over 62 years standing on the crossroads when he has no money, no house and a long way to go, though he has no liability as such. He could have retired from the position of a Chief Engineer, had he continued in his job. His colleagues are today consultants with enough bank balance and their own house. What went wrong then with Rajiv Mehta? It is a matter which needs to be thought about by the people, who are due for retirement or are in the process of planning their retirement.

Let us think about some financial options to invest in securing a peaceful retirement even if one proposes to take up a job or is getting a good pension.

Identify your needs and goals

We all have big changes in our lives that are more or less a second chance. One has to remember that life shrinks or expands in proportion to one's courage.

While planning for finances, we have to take care of our needs and to think as to what is the objective of planning? It cannot be generalised because it will vary from person to person depending upon his or her state of affairs. So many issues will come up. Some may have acquired property and wealth out of inheritance or somebody may have the spouse in business. One most important aspect should be recognised that planning for retirement of any kind is not confined to people from service only, even a business man or professional needs to plan because as you become old, your energy level and earning capacity deplete and irrespective of your profession you feel like having a steady income for your old age. This requires some planning.

Now we will go step-by-step to plan for financial security after retirement and strictly head basis. Let us identify the needs and goals. These are basically:

- Household expenses
- Entertainment
- Travel
- Medical
- Children's marriage
- Children's education

- Business set up
- Purchase of a car
- Purchase of a house, etc.

All the above needs and goals may or may not be applicable in all cases. Identify your particular requirement. Classification of needs and goals is necessary. There is no use of planning your needs and goals unless the same are classified depending upon the requirements and in some cases in anticipation too. The following are some of the important categories.

- ***Recurring short-term need***
  Monthly requirements – household expenditure
- ***Recurring long-term need***
  Yearly/quarterly requirement–LIC premium, premium for medi-claim, yearly vacation expenses, yearly health check-up, etc.
- ***Contingency fund***
  Small medical needs, unplanned travel, etc.
- ***Short-term (less than a year)***
  Planned travel, relative's marriage, son's marriage, buy microwave oven, etc.
- ***Medium-term (1–3 years)***
  Buying a new car, new house, daughter's marriage, etc.
- ***Long-term investments***
  Long-term goals (creation of wealth for your children, etc.)

Quantification is a must

Once you have identified your needs, they need to be quantified in terms of money required. For example:

Rs. 20,000 for needed monthly household expenditure,
Rs. 10,000 as contingency fund

Rs. 5 lac after 3 years to buy a car,

Rs. 35 lac to buy a house after 6 years,

Rs. 5 lac to give to children when they turn 25, etc.

The needs and goals quantified above are as per the valuations of the current market. The money required will increase in real terms with time and you will be requiring more money in absolute terms at that time. For example the goal of owing a house after 3 years may require an adjustment of 15%.

Identify sources of income

Now this particular aspect is applicable for the serving people who are retiring on superannuation with a pension plan. They must keep the following issues in mind:

- Lump sum money received at the time of retirement – ***one time***
- Monthly pension – ***recurring***
- Earlier savings – ***one time or recurring***
- Investments made out of the retirement money – ***one time or recurring***
- Any other income, say from business or agriculture – ***recurring***

Prioritization is necessary

We have discussed identification, classification, quantification and time adjustment of needs and goals but the most important aspect is to prioritize them. You need to have proper thinking as per your individual situation as to how you are going to prioritize. Some of the areas are indicated below:

- ***Protection needs***
  - – Food, shelter, clothing, medical, etc.

- ***Societal needs***
  - Entertainment, marriage, pleasure trips, etc.
- ***Contingency needs***
  - Sudden medical issue, etc.
- ***Specific needs***
  - Upgrading/change of your car after 3 years
- ***Investment needs***
  - Wealth creation, capital appreciation, etc.

Matching of needs is important

The next important step is to match your needs with the sources of income and then arrive at the investible surplus. For example, match your monthly pension with the monthly household expenditure and if the monthly pension amount is higher than the monthly household expenditure, the remaining pension amount may be used to allocate for other needs or it may be marked as an investible surplus.

After your basic needs including household expenditure, medical, contingency, etc. have been matched and fulfilled arrive at the amount remaining, which can be invested to achieve the remaining goals.

Try and match your monthly needs with the monthly/recurring source of income and if the monthly income falls short of the monthly needs then the remaining need may be classified as a recurring need for which investment has to be made.

For example, your monthly pension is Rs. 15000 and the monthly household expenditure is Rs 18000. You need to plan your investments in such a way that you get Rs. 3000 every month uninterrupted and without any risk. So classify Rs. 3000 as a recurring monthly need.

Available investment avenues

This area is quite critical because no perfect advice can be given on the face of changing policies and lots of variations due to budget of the government, various announcements, changes in schemes. Therefore, only a bird's eye view is given here. The following common schemes and guidelines may be kept in mind:

- *Recurring short-term needs*
  - Post office MIS
  - Saving a/c with a bank / post office
  - MIPs of Mutual Funds
  - Senior Citizen's Term Deposit with banks
  - Flexi / Savifix accounts
  - SWP of Mutual Funds
- *Recurring long-term needs*
  - P.O.'s Senior Citizen Savings Scheme
  - Term Deposits with banks / post office
  - QIPs of Mutual Funds
- *Contingency fund*
  - Saving Account with a bank with Debit/ATM Card facility
  - Hard cash at home
- *Funds for 1–3years*
  - Term deposit with bank
  - Gold
  - Balanced schemes of Mutual Funds
  - Blue Chip schemes of MF
- *Long-term investments*
  - Term deposit with bank
  - Life insurance policies

- Equity schemes of Mutual Funds
- Directly into equities
- Bonds
- Real estate
- Commodities trading
- Gold
- Post Office Saving Schemes

If recurring investable surplus is available then invest in the following way:

- Recurring deposits with banks
- RD with post offices
- SIP in Mutual Funds
- LIP with monthly premium
- ULIP

Invest wisely with due care

Start planning from the protection needs and go on to the remaining in order of if any surplus left. List down the alternatives available for each class of needs by comparing the following alternatives:

- Whether investment will be able to give returns in real terms?
- Liquidity
- Risk factors
- Tax implications as per the latest law
- Matching with the needs?

Adopt the ideal investment allocation strategy

You may arrive at a net allocable surplus after taking care of all your needs from which parts could be invested in equity oriented Mutual Funds and rest in low-risk investment avenues keeping 10% funds in liquid instruments, say for example:

If the allocable surplus is Rs. 15 lac and your age is 60 years then Equity will be 30%, i.e. 4.5 lac with low-risk instruments of 60% is 11.5 lacs and finally the liquid of 10%

Think about Term deposit with a bank

Nowadays, there are number of banks – nationalized banks, private banks, cooperative banks and other financial institutions that are authorised to deal in term deposits. They all operate as per Reserve Bank of India guidelines which change from time to time. Still a broad prospective of term deposit scheme especially for Senior Citizens has been given below to give you a general idea:

- **Senior Citizens Scheme**: Individuals above the age 60 can avail Senior Citizens Scheme. Special Hiked Interest Rate is payable to Senior Citizens.
- The depositor can open Fixed-Deposit account called **Senior Citizen Fixed Deposit** account where monthly/quarterly/half yearly/yearly interest is paid. The deposit could be for a maximum period of 10 years. Minimum amount of deposit should be **Rs. 1,000 per deposit receipt** and in multiple of Rs. 1000/- with no maximum deposit ceiling.

  Loan facility: Up to 85% of deposit amount is generally available.
- Some of the banks are providing free ATM Card facility if the customer is maintaining a SB A/c with the branch and free MBB facilities in SB/CA maintained by the customer if the branch is covered under MBB.

Specimen Term Deposit

Maturity Period	Up to Rs. 15 lakh @	More than Rs.15 lakh but less than Rs.1 crore #
07 days to 14 days	4.25	45
15 days to 29 days	4.5	4.75
30 days to 45 days	4.5	4.75
46 days to 90 days	5.25	5.5
91 days to 179 days	5.75	6
180 days to less than 1 year	6.25	6.5
1 year to less than 2 years	6.5	6.75
2 years to less than 3 years	6.5	6.75
3 years to less than 5 years	7	7.25
5 years to 10 years	7	7.25

@ Minimum size of deposit per receipt should be Rs. 1 lakh through single voucher.

A deposit for Rs. 15 lakh and above should be through a single voucher under senior citizen deposit scheme, additional interest over and above card rate will be paid @ 0.50% for the period of less than 1 year, 0.75% for a period 1 year to less than 3 years, 0.50% for a period 3 years to less than 5 years and 0.25% for a period of 5 years to 10 years deposits will be accepted for a maximum period of 10 years.

Post Office Schemes % the safest way

It has been generally observed that though private banks and other financial institutes offer higher interest rate but people still rely on the post office schemes. This is mainly due to the reason that post offices are available even in remote areas and being a pure government sector a retired person feels his money is secure. Some of the schemes offered by post offices are indicated below.

- **Senior Citizens Savings Scheme**
  - 9% interest per annum payable quarterly
  - Age 60 years & above
  - Tax deduction at source @ 10.2%

- Maximum deposit of 15 lac of retirement funds or lower
- Single or joint with spouse only
- Maturity period 5 years
- Extension up to 3 years with interest at prevailing rates
- Nomination facility available
- Premature closure available after 1 year
- Pre mature closure 1-2 years with 1.5% penalty
- Closure after 2 years with 1% penalty
- Transferable with a fee of Rs 5 lac

➢ **Monthly Income Scheme**
- Interest @ 8% per annum
- Rs. 80 monthly for a deposit of Rs. 12,000/-
- 3 lakh in single account & 6 lakh in joint account
- Nomination facility available
- Maturity period 6 years.
- Premature closure after 1 year on 3.5% penalty
- After 3 years – no penalty

➢ **5 Year Recurring Deposit**
- 7.5% interest per annum compounded quarterly
- Account of Rs. 10 becomes 728.90 on maturity
- Nomination facility available

➢ **Time Deposit Scheme**
- 1 year with 6.25% interest per annum compounding quarterly
- 2 year with 6.50% interest per annum
- 3 year with 7.25% interest per annum
- 5 year with 7.50% interest per annum
- No interest if closed within 6 months
- 2% closure penalty for premature closure

Again, we must take into account that all the above

schemes are subject to change and revision, depending upon the policies of the post office. Therefore, these may be taken subject to confirmation by the post office.

LIC policies

Life Insurance Corporation is another government owned body which is highly reliable. The people prefer to take the policies for self and family members and in some cases a LIC policy is also taken for gift purposes. In spite of government liberalization policies allowing private sector to participate in the field of life insurance people still feel more secure with LIC. Some of the common schemes of LIC available are listed below:

✓ ***Endowment Policy with profit***
- Age limit upto 65 years
- Maturity period –minimum 5 years, maximum age of 75 years
- Sum Assured +Bonus at the end of term
- On accident about payable twice the sum assured.

✓ ***Jeevan Anand Policy***
- Age Limit up to 65 years
- Maturity period – minimum 5 years, maximum up to age of 75 years
- Sum Assured + Bonus at maturity
- After death sum assured to nominee
- Accidental risk rider also available

✓ ***Komal Jeevan – ideal policy to gift your children***
- Can be gifted by parents or grandparents
- Child up to 10 years
- Guaranteed additions at Rs. 75/1000
- Premium payable up to 18 yrs or single
- 20% each at 18-20 years

- 30% each at 22 – 24 years
- Maturity at 26 years – approx 1.95 times of sum assured
- Premium waiver benefit.

✓ ***Pension plans of LIC***

- The scheme is announced from time to time; therefore, one must check with LIC about the latest scheme

Mutual Funds as a wise option

The government has given number of tax benefits for mutual funds which keep on changing; still it is one of the most popular investment plans. However, keep the following in mind:

- ***Monthly Income Plans***
  - Around 80% in debt & 20% in equities
  - 7-10 % returns
  - Systematic withdrawal plans
- ***Systematic investment plans***

Property is the best investment

In today's scenario not only in India but all over the world the property prices are sky rocketing. If you look for the investments made in the property you will observe that it has given unbelievable exorbitant return, much above the expectations. One cannot be sure about the rising trend as to how long it will continue but one thing is there that in spite of speculation nowhere a decline has been seen. Especially in metros.

If you have a house it serves many purposes. You can live in your own house and if you have got some extra disposable income, you can construct extra rooms or apartments to be given on rent for a steady regular income.

A lot can be said on this issue but due to uncertain situations it is better to take a decision depending upon the prevailing conditions. There may be a number of advices — somebody might suggest giving the house on rent, another will say on lease and some will say to make it a student's hostel.

For all financial matters consult your life partner and take a decision. That is the best way and don't regret your decision, especially in terms of financial planning, whatever it may be.

Reverse Mortgage as a boon

There is a good news for the people who have got no regular source of income after retirement nor they are getting any employment due to any reason may be on medical grounds or otherwise. The concept of reverse mortgage has come like the name suggest. Normally we mortgage our property to take loan. Here the mortgage is in reverse sense where the property is taken by the bank or a financial institution and equal monthly instalments for the value of property are negotiated between the bank to pay EMI to the property owner.

Say you are retiring and you have no income except your own house to live, then do not worry. Go for the reverse mortgage where the bank will value the property, say to the tune of Rs. 15 lac and as EMI on the particular rate applicable will be calculated say with a rough calculation 10% interest, it may come to Rs.15000/- per month for 20 years. What will happen that you will get Rs.15000/- per month as EMI coming from the bank for 20 years. In legal terms your house will be the bank's property in case all the EMI's are paid to you.

Suppose you and your spouse do not survive for

20 years then your legal heirs, for whom you Will the property, will have the option to own the house after paying the EMI amount with interest due to the bank.

Don't you agree that this is the best retirement plan for retired persons who are incapacitated for having any source of income but are lucky to have a house in their name.

Legal Knowledge—A Must for Everyone

Law is a jealous mistress and requires a long and constant courtship.
It is not to be won by trifling favours, but by lavish homage.

—Joseph Story

G.K. Menon, after completing his graduation in engineering, joined as a management trainee with a leading public sector steel company. With a sound family background, being the only son of his parents he inherited a lot of property. As long as his father was alive, the agriculture property, shops and other properties owned by his father were not his worry. Before dying his father had made a will and got it registered, leaving the entire property to him.

Menon had a passion for acquiring property and tried his luck in the share market often. He was blessed with three sons and two daughters. His children got educated in India but one after another except his youngest son, went abroad and settled there. The properties purchased by Menon were mostly on general power of attorney and he believed in taking over the property on the strength of agreement to sell. Being in government service he wanted to avoid declaration in the annual property returns.

Therefore, he found an easy way out – not to have the title of the property in his name. Moreover, he thought a heavy registration duty would also be saved in this manner. In fact he was doing the property business by sale and purchase of land/flats.

Menon was keeping good health. He was 55 years of age but nobody could say that he was more than 40. Regular exercises and diet control helped him in maintaining good health. He was fond of cars but again he was very careless in getting the registration of the cars in his name. His son was in service with a private company in Kerala whereas Menon was having his empire in Madhya Pradesh. His daughters were married happily and were settled in Karnataka.

Destiny is not in the hands of human being. Man proposes but god disposes. It so happened that one fine morning Menon while driving met with an accident. He became unconscious with multiple injuries and was hospitalized. All sons, daughters and his wife were there on his bedside when he breathed his last. There were so many things he wanted to tell them but only his eyes communicated untold stories.

After the funeral and other necessary religious rituals the family members – his wife, sons and daughters, sons-in-law, daughters-in-law assembled to discuss about the future course. Nobody wanted to say anything about the property matters as long as Mrs. Menon was there. Mr. & Mrs. Menon were the ideal couple. Mrs. Menon was a religious lady, very calm and introvert. Menon never consulted his wife about his property matters, not even the official matters. A lum sum amount of over Rs. 25 lakh was given by the steel company as terminal benefits to Mrs. Menon which was kept in fixed deposits by her younger son. It was about 15 days since Menon expired and all relatives were planning to move to their respective places, when they met with an unfortunate unforeseen incident, which was not anticipated. Mrs. Menon while climbing stairs of the bungalow fell down and suffered brain injuries. She went into coma and expired on the third day in the hospital.

The family members, who were still under shock because of G.K. Menon's death, could not react to this trauma, but it was a harsh reality to be faced by everybody. Some elderly members of the family took the decision to address the children after the funeral of Mrs. Menon. They asked the children to amicably settle the property matters since everybody was eager to leave. They asked about the G.K. Menon's Will. But nobody could say anything since it was not in their knowledge. Everybody hunted for the documents in the safe, lockers and almirahs. What they found was only rent receipts, power of attorneys in the name of G.K. Menon, a copy of the Will of their grandfather and a large number of photocopies pertaining to property transactions. It took time to make the list of properties and other assets in the form of shares, bank accounts, etc. The tenants said that Menon used to take cash from them, issue receipts against them. They did not find any proof of transactions through bank. What followed was a dispute among the children as how to divide the property, deposits, shares, etc. The daughters were not willing to leave their share. The real question remained as to how to take possession of the properties since except the property in the name of grandfather there was no title available for the others. In official records also only the wife was a nominee who had already got the money during her lifetime from the company.

Now look what actually happened. There was no legal document, no declaration of property, no title deeds, no registration of property - not even a proof of payment of municipal taxes by Menon. How to prove the ownership? General power of attorney is not an absolute document. Even the rent agreements were not there because G.K. Menon decided everything with words of mouth and kept the things with him. Some people anticipated a lot of hidden cash which should have been there but where it was kept nobody knew. A state of total confusion was created which resulted in lots of arguments among children. One son engaged a lawyer and gave notices to other two brothers and sisters. The same thing happened from the side of daughters of G.K. Menon.

Now, the question comes, as to who was responsible for all this and why it all happened? People must realise the importance of documentation and the value of registration atleast to have the transparency of transactions and to have the ownership of property in legal terms.

In the above case, nobody can say how long it will take for the legal heirs to claim the property. One cannot ignore the possibility of a big loss of property in the hands of tenants who may be tempted to claim the rights by false litigation. Another question arises as to whether the legal documentation is only for a person who is going to retire or it is for everybody? Because life is uncertain and you do not know when you are going to die? Retirement is fixed but death, though certain, is not known to you.

Let's think about certain legal documents which are essential not only for a person who is retiring but generally for everybody.

Let's understand property

Property in legal terms is designated to those things which are commonly recognised as entities for which a person can claim exclusive rights. The property can be immovable such as real state, land, house, etc. or it could be moveable like cash, jewellery vehicle, copyright, patents, etc. which are considered as intellectual properties.

Property can be transferred by way of sale, purchase, gift, will, mortgage, etc. Land selling and purchase is not an easy task because a lot of legal formalities are involved for the transfer of property. One needs to have ownership rights, non-encumbrance certificate, a clear sketch plan, property tax documents and verified credentials of the property owner.

Documentation not only clarity to personal and official matters but also gives peace of mind.

Some of the documents are listed below:

- Will
- Gift Deed
- Lease Deed
- Rent Agreement
- Affidavits
- Agreement to Sell
- Power of Attorney
- Special Power of Attorney
- Indemnity Bond

Since in majority of cases you will require documentation for property purposes therefore the formats have been drafted for the property. If you want these documents for other purposes suitable changes may be made.

WILL – at your sole discretion

A WILL is the most important document in your life whether you are retiring or not. You feel great pride in possessing something which has been earned by you in the form of movable or immovable property which you can give away as per your own discretion. WILL is an instrument which has been recognized by Indian Succession Act and also by the Muslim Law. It is a legal declaration of intention of the Testator with respect to his property which he desires to be carried into effect after his death. The fundamental idea behind WILL is to dispose of the property as a matter of bequeath. Before making the WILL one should bear in mind that it must be intended to come into effect after the death and it is revocable by the person at any time. The WILL can also be there for appointing executors, creating trust, and for appointing testamentary guardians of minor children, etc.

There is an interesting WILL, a privileged WILL, which is made by a soldier who has completed 18 years of age, employed in an expedition or in actual warfare or an airman so employed or engaged or a mariner at sea. Other than this WILL, all other WILLs are Unprivileged WILL. The Privileged WILL can be oral or in writing. Formalities like signatures and attestations do not apply for Privileged WILL.

The WILL must be a legal declaration of the person who makes it. It can be in respect of the person's self-acquired property having a clear title. It should not have any encumbrances. The WILL must express the desire, or intention to be executed after the death of whoever has made it. A very interesting aspect of a WILL is that one can make any number of WILL but it is the last WILL before the death which matters. The person making the WILL must be of sound mind and make the WILL with free will without any coercion or pressure of anybody. Each page of the WILL should be signed by the person and it should be attested by two known persons in the presence of the Testator. It is advisable that a doctor should be a witness while making a WILL with the remarks that the person was of sound mind in full consciousness at the time of making the WILL.

How to make a WILL

In case you are making a WILL for your property, care should be taken to list out all the details, measurements, location, etc. about the property. Even for movable property like cash, jewellry, vehicle, etc. the full description should be given. There is no stamp paper required for a WILL, it can be on a simple paper. Registration of a WILL is not mandatory, but if you so desire, you can do it.

The question comes as why you should make a WILL? The answer is – for your peace of mind, because you feel relaxed and comfortable that after your death there will be no dispute among the legal heirs. If you are giving away your property for a social cause or charity, you feel a great satisfaction that after your death your property will be used as per your wishes.

In case you have not made a WILL your property will go as per the Succession Acts to your legal heirs, because in any case, the property acquired by you out of inheritance from your parents will go as per the law to your heirs. You cannot make the WILL of a property which is not self-acquired as there is a law of inheritance for Hindus, Muslims, and others.

Do not disclose your WILL during your life time

You may be surprised by reading the above line. But it is a reality. I may tell you the story of an old lady whose husband left behind property worth millions. The husband had made a WILL in his wife's name. After the husband's demise the old lady's children started taking full care of her because she had enormous money in hand as a regular source of income coming from the property. All the children were anxious to keep her because she was extremely generous in spending money. Everybody was taking care of her whether it was the son, daughter, sons-in-law, daughters-in-law, even the grandchildren. The lady was very happy, enjoying love, affection and respect from all.

Unfortunately, one day, the lady fell very ill. Soon her condition deteriorated and she was hospitalised. During her treatment a stage came where doctors were of the opinion that she may not survive. It was the turning point in her life. Her children discussed the matter among themselves and took the decision immediately to divide her movable and immovable property by way of preparing the documents in a legal manner. The signatures of the old lady were taken on all the documents while she was in hospital and immediately distributed among themselves. The suggestion given by some relatives to make a WILL was not honoured because they thought it will take time after the death as no executor can be found out and it will be difficult to have the consent of the lady at this critical juncture.

Fortunately or unfortunately, you may say it was bad luck for the lady that she survived and came out of the hospital in healthy state. The first surprise came to her when nobody came to take her. She was made to understand that there is nothing with her now and she has to live on the mercy of her sons and daughters. The lady survived remaining 10 years of her life each day passing with great difficulty without money. The moral of this real story is that let your WILL be a suspense in the mind of your legal heirs and may just have one close friend who maybe executor and custodian of your WILL in original as a trusted person of your confidence.

Let us have another story which is quite relevant in the above context as to how one should plan one's life in old age with love and affection of their near and dears much away from money. There was an old lady who lost her husband. It was a joint family with three sons and daughters-in-law living in the same house. Unfortunately, the old man was not keeping any money with him since it was a joint family business. The widow was quite intelligent who knew that her daughters-in-law will not care for her unless she keeps some hope alive of a good amount of money to come to them after her death. Every night she would open a big iron chest and then lock it in such a manner that it made enough noise to be heard by the daughters-in-law. This act was repeated by her every night. The daughters-in-law were quite curious as what the old lady does in the middle of the night by opening the big box and then locking it with chain and a strong lock. During informal discussion they came to know from her about huge amount of jewellery in her possession. They could not ask directly but the lady intentionally told them that after her death whatever jewellery is there in the box will go to the daughter-in-law who will serve her the best.

This was the beginning of good days for the old lady. All the three daughters-in-law started showing great amount of respect, love and affection, taking care of her to the maximum. This continued for a long time. One day the old lady died and all the three daughters-in-law rushed to her room in a great hurry. They all were discussing about their role in serving the old lady for getting the maximum share of the jewellery. They could not even wait to search for the keys and broke the lock. To their utter surprise, when the box was opened it had nothing but some stones. They could really realize the game played by the old lady during her life time.

The story cannot be taken as an ideal example to be followed but it teaches a lesson to be smart especially when you know that you have no other recourse except to be dependent on your family. It is not cheating because as parents you have spent your money, time, energies in bringing up your children and otherwise also it is their moral duty to serve you when you are old. Now there are laws to safeguard your interest.

You may like to read the 'Maintenance and Welfare of Parents and Senior Citizen Act, 2007' annexed in the book.

How to make your Will

There is no prescribed format of a WILL. It can be a letter on a plain paper in simple words. However, the only important thing is that it must disclose your desire and the details of the property you want to bequeath. Still for your information and guidance a sample format of a WILL is appended below, which can be modified as per the requirement:

This WILL is executed by,.......................(name) aged.................Son/daughter of.........................resident of..........................hereinafter called the "TESTATOR" in favour of Mr...................son of..............resident of.. hereinafter called the "BENEFICIARY". Both these expressions of BENEFICIARY and TESTATOR shall include their legal heirs successors, legal representatives, administrators, nominees and assigns. That I am the absolute owner of the............. (details of the movable and immovable property to be mentioned).

I hereby appoint Mr...............................son of...........resident of.................... as executor of this WILL. This is my last WILL for the aforesaid Property / Properties and this WILL relate only to the aforementioned Property.

I am making this WILL voluntarily without any pressure, fear, with sound mind and in full senses in favour of Mr......................(mention the relationship or even friendship as the case may be).

The aforesaid Property has been acquired by my own funds and resources and it is my self-acquired property. I am making it clear that I have absolute full rights to dispose off / gift / devise / bequeath this Property to any one I like in my life time. So, I hereby devise, bequeath and leave the aforesaid Property to the said Mr..............., who after my death will get the aforesaid Property transferred and mutated........... (as the case may be)................ in his/her name as owner.

Moreover, this WILL has been read out in the presence of my close relatives, i.e. mother, wife and sons ....(as the case may be) ....and they do not have any objection and have consented to this WILL with no objection. I understand the contents of this WILL since it has been drafted by me.

IN WITNESS WHEREOF I have executed this WILL at........(Place) on .... (day) of ....(month) in the......(year) in presence of following witnesses:

Witnesses:

1. Signatures with Name & Address TESTATOR
2. Signatures with Name & Address

It will be appropriate if the WILL is made in presence of a Doctor who may certify the soundness of mind and health condition of the Testator.

Rest your queries about a WILL

WILL is a very important document not only for you but also for all concerned after your death. While interacting with the people I observed that in spite of a general awareness people have a lot of misconceptions mainly due to lack of knowledge. Therefore, the following clarifications are given which may rest the queries with authentic and legal perspectives about a WILL.

- Preparation of a WILL does not require any legal language. It can be written in any language and there is no specific form or format.
- A WILL need not be typed. It can be written in the Testator's own handwriting or in any other person's handwriting. A handwritten WILL is known as a holograph.
- No technical terms or words are necessary for making a WILL.
- A WILL need not be stamped or written on a stamp paper. It can be written on a plain paper. No stamp duty is payable on a WILL.
- Though the registration of a WILL is not mandatory, however, registration is advisable for the benefit that it will not be lost or stolen and the authenticity may not be challenged. A subsequent WILL can be made in spite of the former one being registered.
- A person can change or revoke his / her WILL as any time; it is the last WILL before death, which prevails.

- It is advisable to write on the WILL that it revokes the earlier WILLS. A Latin maxim says, "*voluntas testatoris est ambulatoria est esque ad mortem*", which means that the WILL of a testator is ambulatory or changeable until his death.
- Persons of any religion or faith can make a WILL; however, a Muslim can make a WILL for only 1/3 of his property since the balance 2/3 will go as per *Shariat* Law.
- In case a person dies without making a WILL then his property will go as per applicable Succession Laws. For example, in case of Hindus, Jains and Sikhs it is in accordance with the Hindu Successions Act 1956, for Christian and Parsees it is as per Indian Succession Act 1925 and in case of Muslims the *Shariat* Law applies.
- The WILL will take effect only after the death of the person making the WILL, therefore, the WILL has no effect, whatsoever, till the person is alive.
- While making the WILL. The Testator should write the names, age and relationships of the persons concern to whom he wants to give the property by way of the WILL, with specific mention as to who will get what. In case, any close relative has been excluded it is advisable to state the reasons so as to eliminate possibility of challenge or contest at the time of execution of the WILL.
- The WILL can be made by any person of sound mind, whether male or female for self-acquired property of any kind.
- It is advisable to have a doctor as a witness to the WILL so as to record that the person is of sound

mind and has made the WILL in full conscious.

- A WILL made under undue influence or coercion is not valid and can be challenged. Similarly, a WILL caused by fraud is invalid.
- The WILL must be signed by the Testator and in case of an illiterate person, duly attested thumb impression should be there.
- The WILL must have a date in order to establish the last WILL.
- The WILL need to be attested by two or more witnesses who may not know the contents of the WILL, however, their attestation will be in testimony that the Testator has signed the WILL in their presence.
- Normally, a person as executor of the WILL can be an attesting witness. It is advisable to have a professional such as a lawyer, a charted accountant or a doctor known to the attestator, as witness.
- The executor of the WILL named by the Testator is responsible to carry out the wishes of the Testator as mentioned in the WILL after the death. The name of the executor should be written by the Testator only after taking his willingness to carry out all the responsibilities. Normally, the executor must complete all formalities of execution of the WILL within a period of one year from the day of the death of the Testator.
- The executor must provide for all funeral expenses of the deceased including death bed charges, medical expenses, etc. and these expenses must be met from the estate of the deceased.
- In case, a probate is taken from the Court the executor and the administrator of the WILL must

produce the inventory of all movable and immovable property and all credits and debts of the deceased to the Court within six months from the date of grant of a probate by the Court.

- The executor or the administrator cannot purchase any property of the deceased, since such a sale is voidable.
- The WILL must be interpreted as a whole and its meaning must be ascertained from the entire instrument, because sometime general words may be understood in more restricted terms than they denote. If the wording of the WILL leads to two meanings and one of them has some effect while the other does not then the wordings which are effective should be given the cognizance and effect.
- Generally, a WILL made by a Testator is revoked after his marriage whether it is a male or a female, because the circumstances undergo a fundamental change after marriage.
- It is not only the first marriage of the testator but every marriage revokes the previous WILL.
- The provisions relating to the revocation of WILL on marriage of the Testator do not apply to Hindus, Sikhs, Buddhist and Jains.

At times people misunderstand the probate with succession certificate. Therefore, it is essential to know that probate is the copy of the WILL certified by the seal of the court which establishes the finality and authenticity of the WILL to validate the acts of the executor. Whereas, a succession certificate is issued by the court when a person dies without making a WILL. Thus, a probate is granted by a court only when there is WILL of the Testator. Whereas, a Succession Certificate is granted when the

WILL has not been made.

Gift Deed

Gift is the transfer of certain existing movable or immovable property made voluntarily and without consideration by one person called the DONOR to another person called the DONEE and accepted by or on behalf of the DONEE. If you are planning to gift the property, you must know that you can gift the existing property not the future property. Your gift should be by way of your free will without any undue influence. The gift has to be without consideration. In most of the cases it can be for natural love and affection or for past consideration. It can-not be for present or future consideration. Another important point is that the gift must be accepted by the donee.

The provision of gift has been made in the Gift Tax Act. Therefore, you must check the latest law governing the gifts with regard to tax applicable. Another thing is that a gift once made and accepted cannot be removed. There may be some stamp duty which needs to be confirmed. A specimen for the Gift Deed is appended here which may be used as a matter of guidance:

THIS DEED OF GIFT is made on this.........(day) of.........(month) ......(year) by Mr./Ms.............. son/ daughter of..............resident of................ hereinafter called the DONOR on one part AND in favour of Mr./ Ms.................son/daughter of................ resident of........................ hereinafter called the DONEE on the other part.

WHEREAS the said donor is the absolute owner of .... (mention details of the movable or immovable property) as the case may be.

WHEREAS the said DONEE is the relative/friend of DONOR for..............................(number) years and the said DONOR has great love and affection for the said DONEE. The donor is desirous out of such natural love and affection of disposing the above-mentioned property to the DONEE.

NOW THIS DEED OF GIFT WITNESSETH AS UNDER:-
That in pursuance of the above facts and circumstances, the said DONOR out of his free will without fraud, coercion or undue influence from anybody whomsoever and in the full possession of his senses do hereby give, convey, grant, transfer and confirm the above property with all privileges, profits, advantages whatsoever attached to the said property gifted unto and to the use of the said donee forever and absolutely.

IN WITNESS WHEREOF the said DONOR is here unto set and subscribes his signatures and delivered in the presence of the witnesses on present day, month and the year first above written.

Witnesses:
1. Signatures with Name & Address

Signatures of DONOR

2. Signatures with Name & Address

Signatures of DONEE

Schedule of Property gifted. Mention specific details of property gifted.

Lease Deed

The lease of immovable property consists of elements like TRANSFER OR as LESSOR and TRANSFEREE as

LESSEE so that both may agree for the transaction. It must be for a certain time or period of duration. The objective of the lease deed is to transfer the rights to enjoy immovable property for some consideration of a price paid or promised.

When you are retiring the lease deed becomes an important instrument for giving your house on rent to have a regular income. You must take care that the things are specific and clear in the lease deed, such as the monthly rent, duration, and the description of the property. The rights and liabilities of the lessor and lessee are also to be made very specific. The process of registration, if required, attestation and stamp duty need to be checked for executing the lease deed.

Rent Control is a state matter which is governed by the laws made by the respective states. The provisions are modified from time to time; therefore, before drafting the Rent Agreement and Lease Deed one must see the relevant acts. The best way is to purchase the latest copy of the Rent Control Act and read the provisions carefully. As a retired person with lot of experience it should not be difficult to understand the various provisions of the Act, because it will save you from any misguidance by interested persons.

Here are the formats for Lease Deed and Rent Agreement for general guidance which can be modified as the need be.

Please do not forget to issue a rent receipt conforming the terms and conditions of the lease deed and rent agreement as the case may be.

A specimen format is given here for your guidance;

THIS LEASE DEED is made on this.........(day) of.........(month) ......(year) at ....(place) between Mr/Ms..............son/dauther of .... resident of....................................... hereinafter called the LESSOR/LANDLORD which expression shall include his/her heirs, successors, legal representatives and assigns, on one part and ....(in case of company) through its Director Mr.................................) hereinafter called the LESSEE/TENANT, which expression shall include his/her heirs, successors, legal representatives and assigns, on the other part on the terms and conditions mentioned hereinafter:

WHEREAS the LESSOR/LANDLORD is the owner of the premises .... (details of property) for which the space specifications/accommodation, fittings and fixtures are described in the schedule annexed hereto.

AND WHEREAS the said LESSEE/TENANT is desirous of taking the said premises on lease together with the furniture and household effects now in the premises for his/her residential use or for Mr................ (name of executive in case it is for the company) and/or his nominee under the terms and conditions mentioned below the said LESSOR/LANDLORD has agreed to give the said premises on lease under these terms:

NOW THIS DEED OF LEASE WITNESSETH AS UNDER: That in consideration of a sum of Rs............... (in figures) (Rupees. ....[in words]) paid by the LESSEE/TENANT to the LESSOR/LANDLORD as refundable security deposit since the sum of Rs. ...... (Rupees......) per month has been agreed as monthly rent in respect of the said premises in consideration of the terms and conditions mentioned in this deed.

The LANDLORD/LESSOR hereby conveys by way

of this lease the said dwelling Property unto the said tenant and has delivered the possession of the same alongwith the furniture or fittings incorporated in the annexure attached to hold the premises unto for residential use or occupation.

THAT the premises with furniture and effects shall be held by the tenant for a tenanted period for ________ year(s) commencing from..............(day) of........... (month) ....(year).

THAT the LESSOR/LANDLORD will issue a valid rent receipt in favour of the lessee/tenant for the rent received by him at the rate of Rs...........(Rupees ....) per month.

THAT the LESSEE/TENANT shall pay all charges for water and electric current supplied to the premises during the tenancy as per the consumption and as per the bills issued in his behalf by the competent authorities.

THAT the house tax and other taxes, charges of assessment of the tenant premises shall be the liability of the LESSOR/LANDLORD.

THAT during the tenancy the tenant shall keep in minor repairs of all the fixtures and fittings in the premises. In case any damage caused to the premises or such fittings and fixtures, etc. it shall get the same repaired at the lessee/tenant expenses within a reasonable time.

THAT the LESSEE/TENANT shall not be entitled to sub-let or assign his interest or the benefit of this deed or part with the possession or the tenanted premises or any part thereof to anybody.

THAT during the tenancy the tenant shall not effect any additions or alterations in the existing structure of the premises without the consent of the LANDLORD/LESSOR in writing.

THAT the tenant shall permit the landlord or his agent at all reasonable times to enter the premises for the purpose of examining the state and conditions thereof.

THAT at the termination of the tenancy, the tenant shall deliver upto the landlord, the premises alongwith all the fixtures or fittings in as good a state of repairs or decoration as the same are now in. Accordingly, the above refundable security deposit will be refunded by LESSOR/ LANDLORD.

THAT the two years tenancy period of this lease may be extended for another period on such terms and conditions as mutually agreed by the lessor / landlord and lessee / tenant.

IN WITNESS WHEREOF the parties to there present have hereunto set and subscribed their hands on the day, month and year first above written.

Witnesses:

1. Signatures with name & address

Signature of LESSOR/LANDLORD

2. Signatures with name & address

Signature of LESSEE/TENANT

Rent Agreement

House rent becomes a good source of income not only after retirement but during the service period also. You may be having company accommodation or two houses. You feel like giving one house on rent. Don't spend money for engaging lawyer or spending money with property dealers. What you need to do is to purchase a bare act of Rent Control Act to know the latest provisions. It is advisable to give the house on rent for a specified period. Now, landlords are fortunate that by virtue of various court rulings it has become easy to get the house vacated.

A format of Rent Agreement is appended below for your guidance;

This Rent Agreement is executed at......(Place) on this...... (day) of ....(month) ......(year) between Mr./ Ms.............aged...........son/daughter of:........resident of.................hereinafter called the "FIRST PARTY" AND Mr./Ms.............. aged.............son/daughter of..............resident of................. hereinafter called the "SECOND PARTY".

The expression of FIRST PARTY and SECOND PARTY hereinafter called and used shall mean include them, their heirs, successors, legal representatives, administrators, nominees and assigns.

WHEREAS the First Party is OWNER/LESSEE of ...... (Property details).

WHEREAS the aforesaid Property is self-acquired Property of the First Party and as such the First Party is fully competent to enter into this Agreement on the following terms and conditions:

NOW THIS RENT AGREEMENT WITNESSETH AS UNDER:

THAT the First Party has agreed to let out the aforesaid Property on rent to the Second Party and the Second Party has agreed to take the same on rent.

THAT the First Party grants and the Second Party accepts the lease of the aforesaid Property for a period of.................years and the Second Party will enjoy the rights, privileges, benefits conferred upon by the First Party.

THAT this Rent Agreement will come into force with effect from....................(day) of.................... (month) ....(year).

THAT the monthly lease rent for the said Property will be Rs...................(Rupees............................) per month of Rs................(Rupees.....................).

That the Second Party has deposited non-refundable security of Rs...........(Rupees.........) to First Party on which no interest will be payable by the First Party vide cheque no............... dated................. drawn on......................... in favour the First Party in full payment of rent for the lease period of First Five years.

THAT the Second Party will have absolute rights to use itself lease hold rights of the premises but will not be allowed to sub-let the premises to any other person for own purposes.

THAT the Second Party will pay house tax, bills of Electricity and water charges or any other dues and demands of the concerned authorities directly to the concerned authorities.

IN WITNESS WHEREOF the First Party and the Second Party have executed this Rent Agreement at the ....(Place), on this ....(day) of ....(month) in the .....(year), in presence of the following witnesses:

Witnesses:

1. Signatures with Name & Address

Signature of FIRST PARTY

2. Signatures with Name & Address

Signature of SECOND PARTY

Receipt for rent

You must be thinking why this heading rent receipt is here. But let me tell you that it is important for you as a landlord or as a tenant to have the rent receipt with you. For the purposes of claiming tax benefit from your employer you need the rent receipt from the landlord. Similarly, as a landlord for showing you income from house property, it is better to keep record of such receipts.

A specimen format of a rent receipt is appended below which can be used for issuing the same to your tenant:

RECEIVED from Mr./Ms...............son/daughter of ....tenant of the house situated at ....(address) the sum of Rs..............(in figures).......................(in words) on account of the rent for the said house for the period from .... to........... @ Rs........ per month.

Dated and delivered on this.........(day) of ...(month) ......(year)

Witnesses:

(Revenue Stamp)
Signature Landlord/
House owner.

General Power of Attorney

A Power of Attorney is a document where a person gives authority to another person to act in his place and instead. It has been defined in the Stamp Act. Basically, Power of Attorney is the delegation of authority in writing by which you empower a person to act on your behalf.

If the Power of Attorney is made general for certain acts it is called a General Power of Attorney and if you appoint a Attorney for a specific Act the deed will be called as a Special Power of Attorney. A Power of Attorney can also be executed by or in favour of two or more persons.

It is advisable to have the witnesses in the deed and it should be attested and authenticated by a Notary Public or a First Class Magistrate. The Provisions regarding Stamp Duty and Registration Act must be checked and complied.

A specimen format is appended below which can be used for the purposes of executing a General Power of Attorney. Necessary modification must be made as per requirement since this format pertains to property transaction.

KNOW ALL MEN BY THESE PRESENTS THAT I, ...(name of executor) do hereby appoint, nominate, constitute and authorize Mr./Ms..............son/ daughter of.............. resident of ....as my true and lawful General Attorney in respect of ....(details of Property, etc.) and I do hereby empower my said Attorney to do the following acts, deeds and things in my name and on my behalf.

To manage, control and supervise the aforesaid property in all respects.

To obtain permission to sell the aforesaid Property from the concerned authority and in this respect to make application, to sign requisite forms and affidavits, to give statements, produce documents, obtain permission under his own signatures.

To sell the aforesaid Property, to execute sale deed to admit the execution, to get the same registered at the time of registration of sale deed, to file affidavit and declarations before the sub-registrar under the provisions of Urban Land (Ceiling & Regulation) Act, under his own signatures.

To give the aforesaid Property on rent, to recover and realize rent, to issue receipt under his own signatures, to the tenant through the process of law or by negotiation.

To get the aforesaid Property transferred and mutated in the name of the purchaser or his nominee, to get the house tax assessed/charged, to get electricity and water meter installed/charged, and act in the office of competent authority, assessor, collector, water department or any other concerned authority, to make appeal before any of the concerned authorities, to sign requisite forms, to file affidavits, undertakings, declarations, to give indemnity bond, security bond, no objection certificate to produce documents, deposit security, house tax, lease money, ground rent, electricity and water charges, or any other dues and demands of the concerned authorities under his own signatures.

To construct, make additions, alterations and repairs, so as to suit the requirement from time to time.

To reply to the letters and notices received from various authorities under his own signatures and follow-up the correspondence in all respects.

To execute deed/perpetual lease deed, transfer deed, or any other document relating to the title of the aforesaid Property in offices of the concerned authorities at the time of registration of any of the said documents before the sub-registrar concerned then to admit execution, present the same for registration and get the same registered and after getting any of the said documents registered then to take possession and delivery of the same.

To reply to the letters and notices received from the office or any other concerned authority under his own signature in respect of the above Property.

To file, prosecute and defend all kinds of suits, petitions, proceedings, reviews, revisions, appeals, affidavits, give statements, make appearances on my behalf in respect of the above Property.

To compromise, compound such proceedings, withdraw them as and when required at the case may be.

To engage advocates, to appoint general or special attorneys in respect of above Property.

To generally do all other acts, deeds, and things in addition to the above which my aforesaid attorney thinks fit and finds it proper to manage and control the aforesaid Property.

I do hereby agree and undertake to satisfy that all acts, deeds and things done by the said attorney shall be binding on me in all respect as if I could do the same or if I were personally persent.

IN WITNESS WHEREOF I have executed this General Power of Attorney at........(place).........(day) of......... (month)......(year)

Witnesses:

1. Signatures with name & address

Signature of EXECUTOR

2. Signatures with name & address

Special Power Of Attorney

You may be wondering that when all powers have been given to an Attorney by General Power of Attorney, then what is the need for a Special Power of Attorney, the answer lies in the title of this power. A General Power of Attorney is given by you to create another identity of yours, and the person to whom you have given GPA must be a very close, trustworthy and important person. However, there may be certain small matters which are specific in nature, where you may not like to bother the person who has been given General Power of Attorney or you do not want to give General Power of Attorney.

Rather you feel like assigning certain specific jobs specially, in the government offices to some other persons individually. Therefore, a Special Power of Attorney can be given as per the following format:

KNOW ALL MEN BY THESE PRESENTS THAT I,..(Executor), aged.............son/daughter of.................... resident of......................do hereby appoint, authorize, nominate and constitute Mr./Ms...........................son/daughter of..................resident of.................... as my true and lawful Special Attorney to act in respect of my Property ....(details of property) and do hereby empower my said attorney to do the following acts, deeds and things in my name and on my behalf:

To reply to the letters and notices received from various authorities under his own signatures in respect of the above property.

To deposit ground rent, lease money, or any other dues or demands of the concerned authorities.

To represent me in the offices of concerned authorities in connection with the matters relating to .... (purpose) for the above property.

...............list out any other act required to be done.

IN WITNESS WHEREOF, I have executed this Special Power of Attorney at.........on........(day) of........ (month)......(year) in the presence of the following witnesses:

Witnesses:

1. Signatures with name & address

Signature of EXECUTOR

2. Signatures with name & address

Indemnity Bond

Let us first understand as to what is Indemnity. It is a contract by which one party called the INDEMNIFIER promises to save the other party called INDEMNIFIED from loss caused by him by the conduct of the indemnifier or by the conduct of any other person.

In an indemnity the indemnifier undertakes to compensate the indemnified for the loss caused to him by the action or inaction of another person. The undertaking may be to pay the amount of loss and it may or may not be backed by hypothetication of property.

Indemnity is different form guarantee so we should not get confused though these two terms look quite similar. In guarantee a guarantor undertakes to fulfill the obligation of the principal debtor on his default whereas an indemnifier undertakes to compensate for the loss. Moreover, in guarantee there is privity between the surety and debtor but in indemnity there is no such privity.

Let us see the format of an Indemnity Bond which is required to be submitted by you in connection with your property and other matters or in the bank for taking loan etc. Though, there are various kinds of indemnity bonds and the form may differ as per request and purpose.

The following format may be used in connection with the purchase of property, say a flat, as indemnity bond to be taken from the seller by you. The contents of the indemnity bond in the format will get clarified as to how this indemnity bond can be used by changing the context for other purposes.

THIS INDEMNITY BOND is executed at......... (Place) on...............(day) of..................(month)......... (year) by me...............(executor) aged..............son/

daughter of..............resident of................................ hereinafter called the FIRST PARTY. In favour of Mr. Ms...............aged...........son/daughter of................. resident of.................................hereinafter called the SECOND PARTY.

The expression of First Party and Second Party hereinafter used shall mean and include them, their heirs, successors, legal representatives, administrators, nominees and assigns.

WHEREAS, the First Party is the owner/lessee of .... (details of property) by virtue of title deed with the description..............................(mention details).

WHEREAS, the First Party has executed the documents such as Agreement to Sell, Special Power of Attorney, General Power of Attorney, Affidavits, Will, etc. so that aforesaid property ....(Property details) may be permanently transferred in the name of Second Party, ...(give details as the case may be).

NOW THIS INDEMNITY WITNESSETH AS UNDER:

THAT the First Party hereby declares that prior to the execution of the aforesaid document the First Party has not executed any other document, whatsoever, in respect of the above property in favour of any other party and neither the First Party will execute any other document in favour of any other party in any manner except in favour of the Second Party.

THAT the First Party hereby undertakes that the action of their attorney relating to said property shall always be deemed retified by them.

THAT the First Party hereby undertakes not to cancel and or revoke any of the aforesaid document now and hereafter.

THAT in case the First Party does not act accordingly as per terms and conditions mentioned herein then the First Party will indemnify all the losses, expenses, and damages suffered by the Second Party or its nominees.

THAT the First Party declares that no other persons including his legal heirs will have any right to make any objection whatsoever at any stage hereafter as all actions have been done with the consent and knowledge of all heirs and successors of the First Party.

IN WITNESS WHEREOF, the First Party has executed the aforesaid indemnity bond at the place, day, month and the year mentioned above in the presence of the following witnesses:

Witnesses:

1. Signatures with name & address

Signature of EXECUTOR

2. Signatures with name & address

Agreement to Sell

A proposal when accepted becomes a promise and every promise forming the consideration for each other is an Agreement. An Agreement enforceable by law is a contract. All Agreements are Contracts which are made with free consent for a lawful consideration and object.

The idea of informing about Agreement to Sell is for the limited purpose to meet out the situation when you are planning to sell your property. This document will become quite handy for you when you are taking some advance before the deal is finally executed for sale of your property by way of sale deed by paying the stamp duty, etc. and registration thereof.

A specimen format of an Agreement to Sell is appended below for necessary guidance which may be modified as per your requirement;

THIS AGREEMENT to sell is executed at .... (place) on..............(day) of...........(month) .... (year) between Mr./Ms......................aged .... son/daughter of .... resident of.....................................hereinafter called the "First Party" AND Mr./Ms..............aged .... son/daughter of.................................. resident of ....hereinafter called the "Second Party".

The Expression of First Party and Second Party hereinafter called and used shall mean and include them, their heirs, successors, legal representatives, administrators, nominees and assigns.

WHEREAS the First Party is Owner/Lessee of Property ....(details of Property).

WHEREAS the aforesaid Property is self-acquired property of the First Party and as such the First Party is fully competent to enter into this Agreement.

WHEREAS the First Party has agreed to sell the aforesaid Property for a sum of Rs..............(in figures) (Rupees...........[in words]) and the Second Party has agreed to purchase the same.

THAT the First Party has received the part of sale consideration of Rs...........(in figures) (Rupees.........[in words]) from the Second Party by way of Demand Draft No......... dated...................... drawn on................ for Rs....................... (Rupees.......................) and Cheque No..................... dated.................... drawn on ....for Rs................... (Rupees..........................) issued in favour of the First Party by the Second Party and remain payable and/or receivable towards the sale deed from the Second Party at the time of handing over the possession.

THAT the First Party is the Owner/Lessee and in possession of aforesaid flat which is being sold by the First Party to the Second Party.

THAT the First Party assures the Second Party that the aforesaid flat is free from all sorts of encumbrances whatsoever such as prior sale, gift, mortgage, litigation and disputes, stay order and attachment, notification and acquisition or any other registered or unregistered encumbrances. If this fact is proved otherwise as a result of which part or whole of the aforesaid flat goes out from the hands of the Second Party and then the First Party will be liable and responsible to indemnify the losses, damages and expenses thus suffered by the Second Party.

THAT the First Party has made it clear to the Second Party that the aforesaid Property will be delivered by the First Party to the Second Party with effect from the date of execution of sale deed and the Second Party will be fully competent to use for self and other and/or utilize it in any manner as it suits them.

THAT the First Party will obtain permission to sell the aforesaid flat from concerned authorities and will execute the sale deed registered in favour of the Second Party or his nominee/or nominees.

THAT the First Party will pay ground rent lease money, house tax bills, electricity and water charges balance installment or any other dues and demands of the concerned authorities up to the date of this agreement and thereafter the same shall be paid by the Second Party in respect of above Property.

THAT the First Party shall deliver all the relevant

original documents of the aforesaid Property to the Second Party.

THAT the First Party will have no objection if the Second Party gets the sale deed registered in his name or in the name of his nominee/or nominees.

THAT the First Party will have no objection if the Second Party requires any other documents from the First Party at a stage hereafter.

THAT the Second Party will pay the cost of the stamp duty, transfer duty, registration fee in respect of the sale deed relating to the said flat which will be executed and registered in pursuance of this Agreement after getting the balance payment of sale consideration.

THIS agreement of sale is liable to be revoked/ terminated in case Second Party is unable to arrange balance payment of sale consideration within a period of........(months) from.........(day) of.........(month) .... (year) for the purpose of sale deed and in that event the amount of Rs...... shall not be refunded by the First Party.

IN WITNESS WHEREOF the First Party and the Second Party have executed this agreement to sell at the place, day, month and year first above mentioned in presence of the following witnesses:

Witnesses:

1. Signatures with name & address

Signature of FIRST PARTY

2. Signatures with name & address

Signature of SECOND PARTY

Affidavit

It is the most common document which is executed for the purposes with regard to various matters, such as passport, ration card, and for submitting to municipal authorities, bank, etc. It is executed on a non-judicial stamp paper for the value prescribed by the state government from time to time. You need to buy the non-judicial stamp paper from the an authorized vendor who will record your name and address in his issue register and will also write the details on the back of the non-judicial stamp paper and put his stamp. Normally, it is valid for a period of six months from the date of purchase for execution.

An Affidavit is basically a statement or declaration in writing made on oath and solemn affirmation setting out certain facts and sworn or affirmed before a person having the authority to administer oath or affirmation, normally, a First Class Magistrate or a Notary Public or an Oath Commissioner, as the case may be.

Affidavits are confined to such facts as the deponent is able of his own knowledge to prove by his belief.

A specimen format of an Affidavit is given described below:

I,......................., aged..................son/daughter of.....................resident of ...., do hereby solemnly affirm on Oath and declare as under:

THAT (state the facts which are required to be declared)

1..

2..

3..

(Signature)
DEPONENT

VERIFICATION

Verified at..........(place) on this........(day) of ....(month).........(year) that the contents of aforesaid affidavit are true and correct with best of my knowledge and belief. Nothing has been concealed, so help me GOD.

(Signature)
DEPONENT

ATTESTATION by first class Magistrate or Notary Public or Oath Commissioner as the case may be.

Family Settlement

The family settlement or arrangement is a sort of compromise in the form of an Agreement between members of the same family intended to be for the benefit of all concerned so as to avoid litigation.

Courts also give effect to a family settlement upon broad and general grounds that its object is to settle existing or future disputes regarding property amongst members of the family. The family settlement ensures amity and goodwill among relations. The family settlement may be recorded in writing as a memorandum and can also be registered as an agreement.

A format of a family settlement between the heirs of a deceased person is given here for guidance. This format can be used for family arrangement by mentioning relevant details. Normally, the need of such settlement arises on the death of the property owner.

THIS FAMILY SETTLEMENT is made on this ....(day) of...........(month)..............(year). In the year...........BETWEEN Mr............aged............son of.................hereinafter called the FIRST PARTY on one part and Ms.................aged.........daughter of............ hereinafter called the SECOND PARTY on the second party and Ms............aged...........wife of............., the widow of Sh.................hereinafter called the THIRD PARTY all residents of ....in the city................(place).

WHEREAS, the said Sh.............. hereinafter called the deceased, died on ....(date) leaving considerable Property, all detailed and described in schedule attached hereto.

AND WHEREAS, the said First, Second and Third Party claim and allege heirship to the deceased in the respective rights and Second and Third Party have also served the notices claiming ownership and possession of the properties left by the deceased as mentioned in the schedule

AND WHEREAS, the First, Second and Third Parties do not have any dispute with regard to their relationship with the deceased. However, they do have their claims for different reasons which are not accepted among them.

AND WHEREAS, on the face of denial of claims of parties by each other over the Property it is evident that the Properties will be lost in litigation. Therefore, on the intervention of friends and well-wishers of the family; the matters have been discussed and accordingly;

THIS SETTLEMENT is made for the benefit of the family generally and for the purposes of avoiding family dispute and litigation whereby the parties are irrevocably bound as below:

THAT the First, Second and Third Party have mutually agreed to have the share in the Property as marked in the schedule as A for First Party, B for Second Party & C for Third Party.

THAT it is further declared and agreed between the Parties that this FAMILY SETTLEMENT ENDS all disputes between the Parties relating to the respective rights and claims in the Properties of the deceased and each Party for the purposes of this SETTLEMENT admits the claim of the other. The notices served in this regard shall stand cancelled and withdrawn.

IN WITNESS WHEREOF, the First Party, Second Party & Third Party have here unto at..............(place) signed this DEED on day, month, year above written.

Witnesses:

1. Signature with Name & Address

Signature of FIRST PARTY

2. Signature with Name & Address

Signature of SECOND PARTY

3. Signature with Name & Address

Signature of THIRD PARTY

Schedule : List of the Properties marked A,B & C

Career Options—A Vast Ocean to Swim in

You gain strength, courage and confidence by every experience in which you really stop to look fear on the face. You are able to say to yourself, 'I have lived through this horror. I can take the next thing that comes along.' You must do the things you think you cannot do.

Rolf Anthony began his career as a brilliant student. Unfortunately in spite of sincere efforts he could not make it to the IAS. This failure never came in his way as a de-motivator rather he made his failure as strength by acquiring higher qualifications. Later he got selected in the private sector as a management trainee. He had the solid base of academics which helped him in acquiring knowledge and skills required to climb the corporate ladder. Though he got exposure by working in different departments of the organisation during the job training. He opted for the department of personnel management although the growth there was not very fast. Maintaining peaceful industrial relations by way of tackling unions became his expertise. Like any other private company his job as personnel officer was not specified, therefore, he offered his services for the legal and administration departments too.

However, having inherited honesty as a value from his parents it was becoming difficult for him to compromise with the corruption in his organisation which led him to think about changing his job. In the private sector Anthony was drawing a good salary, fringe benefits and other perks. The work culture was good. Even a senior executive was addressed by his first name. These things helped Anthony in enhancing his self-esteem and ego in a positive manner. He was respected by the union and proved to be a proactive industrial relations man, a go-getter opinion leader. Unfair labour practices are quite common in the private sector and his organisation too had its own share in it by way of giving bribes for bypassing various legal requirements relating to labour welfare. At times Anthony felt suffocated for compromising with the voice of his conscience which made him to think of changing his job. So he sat for All India competitions and was selected in some of the public sector companies. He joined one of them as Assistant Manager.

Public sectors have their own rules, regulations, pay scales, etc. which are not comparable with the private sector. Moneywise, Anthony was a loser but somehow he felt satisfied for being able to come out from the suffocating atmosphere of corruption and exploitation of the labour class. The public sectors in the country in the 70s were not at all professional, especially in the field of personnel management. The organisations were run on the old pattern of central government and the personnel department was nothing more than a department of administration. It was being run by promotees from the clerical cadre. There was a great opposition to induction of Rolf Anthony in the organisation as he was an outsider and not an internal candidate.

While working at different units Anthony performed very well and achieved certain milestones. The performance appraisal system in the organisation was not having any objectivity. Therefore, the exemplary performance of Anthony was not reflected in his annual appraisal reports. But Anthony was satisfied and content because of his pro-labour attitude, cooperation with the unions and because his counselling skills were appreciated by all. He initiated new projects, gave emphasis on training and showed remarkable inter-personal skills. He acted as a crusader against corruption which was not objected to but at the same invited the displeasure of dishonest bosses, which harmed his performance appraisal in the form of getting average ratings. The performance appraisal system in the organisation was quite unilateral and career of the executives was in the hands of immediate bosses. The annual confidential reports used to be written at the whims and fancies of the boss. Anthony was fortunate to have some outstanding reports also when he worked under directly recruited professionals. His bosses coming from the clerical cadre suffered with great amount of inferiority complex and always tried to spoil his career prospects.

Anthony witnessed a number of ups and downs during the long period of over two decades in the public sector. He could rise up in the ladder of hierarchy whenever he could prove his merit in the competitions. However, when it was a question of stepping up strictly on the basis of performance appraisal reports he lagged behind. His honesty, straightforwardness and sincerity towards the organisation invited lots of controversies and he was given unpopular postings.

There was a sea change, however, when the open policies of the Government allowed foreign direct investment. A lot of multinational companies came to India and public sectors were also getting privatized. In some cases joint ventures came into existence with public and private participation. There was a boom in the Information Technology (IT) sector. The compensation management with regard to salary and wages got a new trend since it was strictly based on performance. The performance management developed the concept of competency mapping and 360 degree appraisal. Profit sharing gave rise to higher pay package to the executives in multinational companies. Rolf Anthony always weighed himself in the market by applying in the private sector with no intention of joining there. As a matter of fact, he wanted to know his market value, i.e. why he used to make attempts to be successful and unsuccessful also in the selection process.

Anthony was in the process of planning his retirement at the age of 55, when the government policies attracted the organisation where Anthony was working and some of the units of his organisation got privatized. A large number of dynamic executives joined the private sector mainly due to very high package being offered to them. Though the nature of work was the same but the job description and performance appraisal was having new dimensions. The executives who joined the private sector got very high packages to the tune of 35 lakh per annum as compared to Rs. 12 lakh in the public sector.

Being a professional, having a wide exposure and a well read man, Anthony was aware of the happenings and was analyzing the situation, its pros and cons from different angles. When Anthony was still aspiring for the position of General Manager in the public sector with due seniority, his colleagues in the private sector already reached to the level of senior vice-presidents with a much higher pay package.

Undecided about the situation Anthony applied for a senior position in the private sector on the strength of his academics and long experience gained accordingly. He successfully underwent the various stages in the selection process and found himself in the horns of a dilemma when he was reaching the final stage. The package offered to Anthony was to the tune of Rs. 32 lakh per annum. Anthony calculated his salary and after commuting all the perks and facilities offered by the public sector came to the conclusion that his existing package is only 12 lakh per annum. Anthony was confused and was not able to resist the temptation of a high salary package. At this stage he had the occasion of interacting with some of his colleagues who had joined the private sector. It was a matter of great surprise for him when he was told that the private sector working was rashly different with regard to organisational culture. The concept of management by objective for appraising performance was being practiced. It was totally a result-oriented performance management and the employer was not in the habit of getting a NO from the employees. The principle was to beg, borrow or steal to achieve targets. It was 12 working hours with six days a week as compared to 8 hours per day with 5 days a week in the public sector.

Anthony learnt in his life to solve the industrial relations problem by applying pro-active techniques analyzing undercurrents and dialogue with the unions. He had a long experience of sorting out difficult issues by the application of his communication skills and leadership qualities. But he was made aware that things have changed. Since the top management in the private sector will not have patience to wait for the results testing the skills to solve the problems. Honesty was no more a value and it was money to be made by hook or by crook. Anthony was told that in case he decides to join the private sector he should be prepared to change his thinking pattern. Corruption and bribes should not be an issue in his mind. He should only remember about the work and the results. The freedom of speech should also have some brakes since he will not be allowed to call a spade a spade.

Anthony was in a dilemma about the second career as many questions came to his mind.

1. Should I join the private sector for a higher pay package?
2. Will it be possible for me to change my value system?
3. Is honesty still the best policy?
4. Let me continue. I will postpone my retirement planning.

The above is based on a true situation. You may find yourself in a similar position to change the job even prior to your retirement age. There is no harm in planning a second career when good prospects are available. I know a couple of my bureaucrat friends who resigned from the Government and joined the private sector. It is all a matter of thinking whether you give priority to money and being able to have a change in your mindset or you may land up in a situation like Rolf Anthony.

You need to think about the pros and cons

The main question is as to whether you want to take up a career again after retirement or you want to start your own business or you want to do some social service. It all depends on you. Some people may feel like enjoying life without work. But I do not know whether one can enjoy without work. However there are cases where people just kill time reading newspapers or sleeping and not doing anything but simply living on their pension or house rent or bank interest.

I may be addressing this issue to the people who have got responsibilities of marrying the daughter or son or the education of their children. For them, it is a necessity to take up the job so as to have the same amount of money what they were getting before retirement as salary.

The reason why most people never reach their goals is that they don't define them, or even seriously consider them as believable or achievable. Winners can tell you where they are going, what they plan to do along the way, and who will be sharing the adventure with them.

How to make your profile?

There are admirable potentialities in every human being. Believe in your strength. Learn to repeat endlessly to yourself. It all depends on you no matter what the situation.

The question of making your profile at this stage may be sounding funny because normally a bio-data or curriculum vitae (CV) is prepared when you are young and looking for a job. There is a standard format for it which gives your personal details, qualifications, hobbies, etc. Then what is new about addressing this question? Yes, there is, because at this stage you are not making your CV but writing your profile. Therefore, your CV for a second career is going to be different from the usual CV, mainly because t it is your experience you are going to highlight. You do not have time now to acquire more qualifications. In any case it will not be so useful also.

Before making your CV you must be clear in your mind as to what kind of job you can do now and who your prospective employers are, carefully understand the job requirement and job description where you are applying. Accordingly, highlight your expertise by way of similar assignments you have undertaken during your career. It is very difficult for a retired person to remember all the important assignments and achievements during the long tenure of 30 years or so. But it is not impossible. My piece of advice is to think about it for a week. Divide your career span into brackets of 2-5 years right from the beginning of your career till date. Write down the important assignments you have undertaken and the recognitions you have received during your career. Your spouse will perhaps help you in recollecting. You cannot forget the places and the events because birth of your children, the time and energy devoted for their admissions will be a ready reckoner. Let it be one page record of your experience which will be in a descriptive form. Now you need to summarise it in a single line point-wise in such a manner that the prospective employer may find it eye-catching suiting his requirements.

Let us assume that you are a man from finance and worked in various units of the finance department of a large government organisation where you never had the chance to acquire proficiency and expertise in a particular discipline but you have sufficient knowledge of financial matters. After retirement you found an opening where a private firm requires a finance personnel to maintain their books of accounts. Here, comes your useful experience with various units where you had the occasion of maintaining accounts. Highlight the profile of your company and enlarge upon the jobs you had undertaken relevant to the requirements of the company.

Another example can be of an engineer who had been working in a construction company having a wide knowledge of procurement, quality control, tender negotiations and maintenance jobs. A private construction company requires a civil engineer for supervision. Now, your experience in different fields of construction will become relevant and you can make your CV highlighting the relevant aspects which are needed by the private company.

You can become a teacher

It has been observed that teaching is one of the best professions after to take up retirement, even if, you have not retired from an academic institutions, thanks to the requirement of practicing managers in the mushrooming business schools of India. The only essential requirement is your basic qualification. If you have the right kind of aptitude for teaching and also interest, which you may have observed while teaching your own children, acquiring higher qualification is not a big deal today, what with e-learning, distant mode of education, etc. You will not even realise when you have become an MBA and did your PhD.

The most fortunate part is that your industry experience is being equated to a teaching experience by the business schools when they consider you for the job. There is a scarcity of good faculty and most of the institutes are welcoming retired personnel for part time faculty and sometimes full time faculty also. Look for your stream whether it is Marketing, Personnel or Finance. A hardcore engineer may go for operations research and systems, etc. In teaching there is no age of retirement, because you continue as a professor or consultant or adviser as long as you are delivering goods and your health is fine. We shall discuss health in a separate chapter on 'Health Planning', later in this book.

I do not want you to waste your time in making curriculum vitae for different professions because at this stage you are not applying for a job rather you are looking for an assignment on the strength of your long experience. You need to see the requirements of your prospective employer and then design your profile accordingly, in order to ensure that you are not only suitable but also competent enough to perform the job.

Make your hobby as profession

It seems that people have a vast potential. They can do extraordinary things if they have the interest, confidence or courage to take the risks. Don't be surprised to have this idea of making your hobby as your profession after retirement. As a matter of fact, I want to make a suggestion that even before a decade of your retirement, you can plan to choose a job which was your hobby or choice in life but remained unfulfilled all through your career. I would like to name three professions in this regard – a lawyer, professor and doctor. Can you really do it? Of course yes, thanks to the mode of education learning and various e-learning processes.

When you are nearing 50 think about joining a course to acquire a qualification in the field of homeopathic medicine or ayurvedic or Unani therapies from a recognised institute which allows to have the medical qualification making you entitle to have registration as a medical practicenor.

You may have a hidden desire all through your life to be a lawyer, specially if it was your hobby to counsel people, rendering advice to them with whatever legal knowledge you acquired from different sources. Just think of becoming a lawyer after your retirement. There are courses available after which you can get a degree in law. It will not take very long to pursue this qualification and you never know when the years have passed and you have the required qualification which may entitle you to apply for enrolment with the bar council as an advocate.

Now comes the profession of a professor which is already discussed but I need to reiterate that it has got a great demand in the present scenario, thanks to mushrooming of business schools in all big cities imparting regular, part time and correspondence courses to the students and also to the executives who are desirous of obtaining this qualification. Again, you need to check your aptitude as to whether you love teaching. Have you taught your children? What was your experience like? Did you like teaching? If your answer is yes, then you may enrol as a student for acquiring the qualification. You can choose your areas of specialisation also. Age is no bar, because you will find a number of senior executives teaching in the business school.

Nowadays, for considering a candidate for the job of a professor or director of a business school the post-qualification experience in the industry is equated to teaching experience as an academician. It is really a boon for you to have a passion to teach in a business school after retirement. Practicing managers are in great demand as part time and visiting professors. Moreover, the retirement age for a professor may go up to 65 years. There is, therefore, the possibility of a regular job with pay and perquisites after retirement in a profession of your choice.

It is never late to start a business

Recently, while interacting with some senior officers who were due for retirement, I was surprised to hear from one of them that he was going to open a restaurant in his home town in the North-East. When I asked him whether he had any experience in this field, he laughed. His reply really convinced me when he said that he was basically a manager and for running the restaurant he was going to engage people having expertise in different streams of business. The finances were available with him and he was not averse to taking loan. Most interestingly, I could see how his face lit up when he told me that it was his dream in the initial stages of his career to open a restaurant of his own. Since then he has been nurturing the idea of opening one after his retirement, he wants to crystallize those dreams into reality. You may be one such person. So why don't you think in that direction?

Why to confine yourself to a particular business. There can be so many different business options. The most popular being a consultancy firm in the area of your specialisation. You may also enter into property dealing, liaisoning and even start a recruitment agency. May be your son is already into business and wanting the services of a person like you. Why not help him running his business. You may be able to look after the affairs of the company with a sense of ownership with the feeling that you are helping your son.

Start a non-government organisation (NGO)

In the earlier days there used to be limited organisations at the global level doing community service for the welfare of people, for instance, UNESCO, Spastic Society of India, Child Rights & You, World Health Organisation, etc. But in the last two decades there has been a lot of awareness and willingness of people to serve mankind. Today people want to work in the areas of child education, anti-drugs anti-AIDS, poverty elimination, literacy campaigns, food, clothing & shelter for the poor, prevention of immoral traffic, wildlife protection, anti-pollution campaigns, preservation of the environment and so on, with the result that a large number of non-government organisations (NGOs) have opened. A number of national and international bodies associate themselves with these NGOs. The participation in these welfare activities is not exclusively the domain of retired people since the younger generations too are opting this as a career. There are examples where bright IIM postgraduates left a lucrative career with MNCs and joined hands with NGOs or started one on their own.

My idea of giving a brief background about NGOs is to suggest as to why you should join an NGO of your choice or start an NGO. In any case, it all depends upon your preference for a second career and your immediate requirements. The target group for joining an NGO will be people who have got enough money with no commitments and liabilities. It is not necessary that you may join an NGO or start an NGO because basically the idea is to do social service to help people who are in need of help. I am not touching the religious organisations because that is to be taken up separately when I talk about spirituality.

Know Health—No Tension

You don't stop laughing because you grow old.
You grow old because you stop laughing.

Denzil D'suza was working with a multi-national company in a senior position. As a man with an engineering background he was known for his technical skills not in India but in other countries too. Travelling to new places was a part of his job and it was a lavish style of living with imported cars, bungalows, servants and club life which made him an addict of liquor, smoking with vices of womanising and gambling too. He had by-pass surgery of his heart at the age of 50 and suffered with kidney problem. His sedentary life made him to put on weight which seemed okay since he had a good height. He never used to exercise for giving excuses such as having a busy work schedule, which never allowed him time even for a morning walk. Denzil was fortunate to have the best of medical treatment. Regular medical check-ups helped in keeping him to lead a normal life but with the help of medicine.

Denzil never heeded the advice of his family members and other well-wishers to quit drinking and smoking. He never felt the need for reducing weight. Eating at odd hours and taking rich diet made him the victim of acidity and high blood pressure. Again he found solution in the form of pills prescribed by his doctors. He did not plan for retirement mainly because his children were settled abroad and his wife had her own export business. A stage came when doctors advised him to leave drinking since his liver was getting affected. Still Denzil believed in money power. It led him to a situation where he had to go for a kidney transplant at the cost of Rs.15 lakh. Denzil was not alarmed because of his firm belief that nobody can reduce or increase the age, it is in the hands of God. He always believed in living life as it comes. Years passed but there was not much deterioration in his health because of proper medical care. Sometimes his subordinates used to advise him for physical exercises, a sugar free and fat free diet, also to leave drinking and smoking. But as usual he did not heed such advices.

On the day of his retirement Denzil never knew what he was going to do next day. He thought of enjoying life as before with no work. Now he spent time in smoking, drinking, playing cards, gossiping in the club and other such activities. There was no problem of money. He had a regular source of income from shares, rentals, interests from deposits, dividends, and so on.

It was a sad day in the life of Denzil when he found himself in the hospital for treatment of another kidney for which doctors were contemplating replacement. He was put on dialysis and after a few days he was released from the hospital. His stay in the house was for a limited period because of infection which he developed in his system. It became a regular affair for Denzil to be in the hospital for dialysis. He was bed-ridden for all practical purposes. He lost weight and developed the problem of diabetes. His heart was already weak. He was advised not to smoke and drink. The spicy and fatty food was also prohibited. It was not by choice but compulsion that the food was like medicine for him. He was living at the mercy of nurses and caretakers. His people hardly visited him.

Denzil is now 65 years old, it is almost 5 years since he retired. But what a life he is leading? Why did it all happen? Was it because of lack of planning? These are some of the questions which should come in the mind of everybody a decade before retirement or else it will be too late to plan for health. In case you are not alert in your late 40s. How will you go about it? Let us discuss.

No health coverage for elderly

In most of the advanced countries of the world social security schemes are launched for every citizen right from the beginning of his or her career in order to ensure that there is health insurance for them when they have no source of income. Unfortunately, in India, there is no such scheme. Though the government hospitals are claiming to provide medical facilities at a very nominal cost but in reality a poor man in the old age is unable to avail the so-called facility.

Even in the metros, the government provided acres of land at throwaway price to private hospitals with the provision to earmark certain number of beds and free fund treatment for people who are poor. But these hospitals, on acquiring land, are built multi-speciality hospitals with five star facilities, forget their duties towards poor. These hospitals are run by the business groups and not by the doctors. Foreigners are being attracted by them in the name of medical tourism. The sole purpose of the government is defeated.

Most of India's over 80 million senior citizens, both men and women, over 70 do not have health insurance. In a survey undertaken by an NGO across the country over 2000 elderly people were interviewed and it was revealed that only 13% of them had a health cover. This survey covered not only the metros–Delhi, Mumbai, Kolkata, Chennai–but also cities like Vijaywada, Ahmedabad, Lucknow, and Bhubneshwar. It was surprising to find that 87% aged people were not having any health cover whatsoever in case they fell ill, specially, when 42% out of them were already suffering from chronic ailments like hypertension, arthritis, diabetes, etc. The findings of the survey are quite alarming because they indicate that about 62% elderly people do not consult doctors and mostly take medicines at their own discretion or on the advice of the chemist.

In most of the cases, elderly people are dependent on their children for medical and other expenses. In our country the population of elderly people is expected to increase to 135 million by 2020 and as per statistics it will be reaching 324 million by 2050. But still there is no awareness for health insurance. Even in private companies health cover is taken for the employees till the age they retire. If we analyse the findings of this survey conducted in the year 2007, a small percentage of elders was there in metros, say about 15%, who had taken insurance cover. The elderly people expressed their desire to have the health cover in the form of insurance. More than 50% males and females who were having health coverage fall in the age group of 60-69 years. It was the children who were considered responsible to take care of medical expenses for the elders. Out of over 2000 elderly people covered in the survey, 25% showed a sense of insecurity, and majority of them were over 80 years of age.

The idea behind telling the above survey findings is

to make you aware about the purpose and far-reaching benefits of medical insurance. Even the incometax laws are liberal in giving tax benefit for the premium paid on health insurance. In case you are employed and your company is providing medical insurance then take care to get the period of insurance enhanced beyond the age of retirement because the premium is directly proportionate to your age, less age less premium, more age more premium.

Good health is in your hands

The great secret which all old people must share is that they haven't changed in 70 or 80 years. Your body changes but you don't change at all. Some people believe that there are certain body ailments which come by virtue of heredity, such as diabetes, obesity, heart problems, asthma, Parkinson's diseases, etc. But these are all lame excuses. Good health is in our hands. I may be allowed to say that beginning for planning good health start from childhood. Good habits in the form of sports, yoga, meditation, balanced diet added with sleeping habits in the form of early to rise, early to bed support health.

Let us accept that you had no health planning in your youth and now, you are in your late 40s to think about your retirement. It's only a decade ahead. What can you do? Well, a lot can be done even now, if you are not keeping a good health, or you may have some bad habits too.

Water is like air to life

You all know that without oxygen, we cannot survive. It is our life. Similarly, water is also essential for our body. What is new about it, you may say. Yes, it is there. I am making a recommendation for drinking water empty stomach. In some countries like Japan it is taken as a treatment for disease. Keep water in a copper jug at night and immediately after waking up every morning drink as much quantity as you can. You may start with one or two glasses and increase it to 5-6 or more. You may brush your teeth, clean the mouth after drinking water, but do not eat or drink anything for 45 minutes. After breakfast, lunch and dinner do not eat or drink anything for 2 hours, not even water.

This habit of drinking water on empty stomach can cure and prevent a large number of ailments such as headache, piles, diabetes, constipation, asthma, etc.

We do not take enough care of our body till the time we are sick to show to the doctor. Whether you are old or young everybody needs to be healthy. Each and every organ of the body is important and we need to take care of our health in totality. If I start talking about each organ of the body it will not make any sense. Therefore, I will confine my advice to some common ailments.

Heart – a key organ

You may not know that heart is such a unique organ of the body which starts functioning as early as two months in the womb. The entire development of the foetus takes place in phases except function of the heart. All organs of your body take rest except the heart. It is the strongest organ and is meant to work continuously till our last breath. On the other hand, if you don't take care of your heart, it may become the cause of your death. If you are not having a healthy lifestyle it may lead to problems of the heart. There is no age for heart failure. It all depends how much you take care of your heart. More than 60%

people nearing the age of retirement suffer heart attacks. Being overweight, smoking, high blood pressure, high fat contents in the blood and diabetes are some of the causes of heart attack. Regular exercises, a healthy diet and moderate or abstinence from drinking protect the heart.

You must have knowledge about the common symptoms of heart ailments. It is necessary to be rightly informed rather than panic at in slightest chest pain or discomfort. In case you have a family history of heart ailments it becomes important to be alert about symptoms.

Look at the following situations:

- If you feel pain in the chest when angry or while climbing stairs then it is a genuine cause for concern.
- It is also a matter of concern if the pain occurs in the centre of the chest.
- If the pain starts from anywhere between the neck and the upper abdomen. Do not neglect it.
- Sometimes the pain can travel down to the arms. In some cases to the left or the lower jaw. This pain can be associated with the heart.
- If the pain starts from the fingertips of your left hand and move towards the elbow and further upward it can be a sign of angina. It requires immediate medical attention.
- If you feel a peculiar kind of sensation in your entire body accompanied by sweating even in winters and also have feeling of collapsing, it can be a symptom of heart attack.
- For men who have crossed 25 with a waistline of more then 36" and woman who has crossed 35 with a waistline of over 32", they are prone to heart attack or ailment.

If your blood pressure is more than 130/80 and there is a family history of diabetes and heart problem and cholesterol level is also high then you are leading towards the risk of heart attack. The remedy is to have serious changes in lifestyle.

Please keep in mind that your blood pressure should be 130/80 mmHg. If you are not above 50 years a systolic pressure of over 140 is dangerous. The systolic BP of 120-139 and diastolic BP of 80-89 should be considered as pre-hypertensive and you should seriously opt for lifestyle modification.

Here are 10 important tips to keep your heart healthy:

1. Exercise regularly atleast 30 minutes a day which may include yoga, breathing exercise (Pranayama), and most importantly meditation. While exercising, do a combination of aerobic exercises such as brisk walking at a speed of at last 4 km/hrs.
2. Keep your weight in control proportionate to your height. For men, the waist/hip ratio should be less than 0.90-0.95 cm and for women 0.83-0.90.
3. You must abstain from tobacco consumption.
4. Depression, stress, hostility and anger are poison for you.
5. Avoid full cream milk and excessive red meat. Use olive, soya bean or mustard oil for cooking.
6. Make it a habit to have seasonal fruits and green leafy vegetables as part of your diet.
7. Drink plenty of water all through the day.
8. Alcohol consumption should be restricted to two small drinks a day. If you are a habituated drinker

develop taste for cocktails such as screw driver which contains alcohol as well as juices and lime cordial.

9. Regular intake of almonds and nuts is also helpful.
10. After attaining the age of 35 years a complete health check-up is a must every year.

Rule of 100 - a boon for healthy heart

They say, prevention is better than cure. It is an old adage but nevertheless time true, especially when it comes to protecting your heart. The number 100 is important to be remembered for the following:

- Keep your LDL cholesterol (which is considered "bad") around 100 mg /dl. High density lipoprotein HDL is considered as "good" cholesterol which should be over 45 mg/dl for men and over 55 mg/dl for women
- Keep your triglycerides levels around 100 mg/dl or atleast <150 mg
- Maintain a systolic blood pressure around 100 mms/Hg or atleast <130 mm/Hg
- Your fasting blood sugar should always be <100 mg

Remember that your consistent efforts to modify your lifestyle are the only way to prevent a heart attack.

Heart disease - some alarming facts

Heart diseases in India kill more people then AIDS, TB and cancers–all put together because Indians have a genetic pre-disposition towards heart diseases. A study was conducted of Indians living in USA, UK, Singapore, Canada and other places abroad in comparison to the natives of these places and it was found in the same environmental conditions, that Indians suffered from heart diseases 4 times in number as compared to other ethnic groups with higher or similar cholesterol levels. Another study revealed that Indians are 8 times more prone to heart diseases than the Chinese and a startling 20 times more prone to heart problems than the Japanese.

On the face of the above conditions the matter was taken up by a number of researchers and some surprising facts came to light which are quite alarming for India.

- 3 million people die of cardiovascular diseases, e.g. stroke, etc.
- 30% of all deaths are caused by cardiovascular diseases.
- 5 million people will die of cardiovascular diseases by 2020.
- 50% death due to heart ailment is of people under 70 years of age.
- 10% people aged 20 in urban India have cardiovascular diseases.
- 32 million people have diabetes.
- 70 million people will have diabetes by 2025.
- 118 million people have hypertension or high blood pressure.
- 213 million people will develop high blood pressure by 2025.

The above findings are quite surprising but on the face of prevailing lifestyle, food habits and environmental pollution in the country it forces us to believe that this unfortunate situation cannot be overfed unless remedial actions are not taken in time.

You must be thinking why so much emphasis is given to the heart when other body organs are also important.

The answer lies in the question itself because heart is considered as the most important organ of the body. One can live with other ailments but heart failure signifies death.

Asthma

Although, studies revealed that in majority of the cases asthma is genetic but in the present scenario, pollution is the main cause. Even a healthy person with no family history of asthma can develop it. Today, a large number of medicines are available for controlling or alleviating asthma if, not curing it. The best way is still to remain careful during change of seasons. You need to avoid pollution and don't hesitate to take medicine but only after consulting a doctor.

Body-ache

When I use the term "body-ache" my purpose is to include all kinds of pains in the body be it joint-pain, headache, pain in the knee, etc., mainly because of the reason that causes are the same and to some extent the remedies also. Have you ever thought why you suffer the body pain as you grow old? Just think! If you have not been exercising in your young age, it is going to lead to body-ache when you become old, because your body is not going to remain forever.

When you reach 40 years of your age let it be an alarm to do exercises and also taking brisk walk for 30 minutes every day. If you can do yoga and meditation it is best. You must ensure that there is an exercise involving each part of the body, be it the neck, the arms or the abdomen, etc. As far as possible do not take pain killers, as regular use of pain killers may affect the kidneys.

All is well when the stomach is well

It has been observed that most of the diseases are caused by poor food habits affecting the digestive system. Therefore we need to have some guidelines on diet. The National Institute of Health, USA, and the American Diabetes Association have suggested some guidelines for the prevention and control of various ailments. These include weight reduction and lipid regulation. It is useful to a glance at these guidelines:

1. Fat consumption per day .... less than 30% of energy
2. Saturated fat .... 7 to 10% of energy
3. Complex carbohydrates..................35 gm per day of fibre (50% from fruits and vegetables)
4. Dietary cholesterol...........................less than 300 mg per day
5. Unsaturated oils.....................................Mono 10 to 15% of energy / poly (PUFA) 7-10% of energy
6. Increased use of high protein foods

A healthy diet is one way to get started on your health management programme. Let's have a diet list which is based on the guidelines from various medical institutes and health associations. A great emphasis is given for avoiding overeating. You need to keep the following diet list in mind to ensure perfect health.

- Fresh fruits and green leafy vegetables should form a large part of diet.
- Be sure to have one citrus fruit a day.
- Choose vegetables which are more fibrous.
- Chapati, roti and parathas to be prepared with little fats.

- Choose lean meat (like chicken) or fish, boiled, baked or grilled.
- Have egg whites (use freely) but limit yolk to three per week.
- Vegetable oils rich in poly-unsaturated fatty acids (PUFA) like sunflower, kardi, soyabean and sesame are preferable, if you must use oil. Soft margarine may also be used.
- Take fresh fruit juices, black coffee and tea, soft drinks with sugar substitutes and milk beverages made from skimmed milk.
- Have cakes without icing or cream, puddings and ice-cream made with but have in limited or moderate quantity.

Medicine - the last resort

When I went to Switzerland, Singapore and Malaysia and interacted with the people there, I found that the way we Indians take self-medications nobody can believe it in other parts of the world. In fact there you can't purchase medicines without prescription, and even medical stores are quite rare. When I went to a Mall looking for a medical store, I could find only general medicines like aspirin, etc. In India, we do not hesitate to take antibiotics at our own discretion without consulting a doctor. Our sole purpose is to get immediate relief.

A stage has come when a chemist does not hesitate in giving you steroids without knowing the harmful effects of them on our body. In foreign countries, it is impossible to have antibiotics on your own. The doctors are all attached to hospitals and I could not find doctors clinic like we have in India. I realised that there are many reasons for this. Some of the reasons you can find in the above illustrations where emphasis is given on healthy diet and a pollution free atmosphere.

Now, you are retiring, you cannot afford to perhaps buy allopathic medicines always, which are quite expensive. In India, alternative therapies like Ayurvedic, Unani and Homeopathic are easily available and are harmless. But I would like to go one step further and suggest naturopathy unless your problem is very acute. Naturopathy believes in curing ailments and remaining healthy through intake of fruits, vegetables and grains. Let us try and take the benefit of vegetable and fruit juices if we are suffering the ailments.

Arthritis	:	Sour cherry, spinach, cucumber, beet, lettuce, pineapple, lemon, apple and grapefruit
Allergies	:	Apricot, beet, spinach, carrot and grapes
Acne	:	Potato, pear, plum, cucumber, grapes, spinach and tomato
Acidity	:	Grapes, mosambi, carrot, orange and spinach
Arteriosclerosis	:	Grapefruit, lemon, carrot, pineapple, lettuce and spinach
Anemia	:	Spinach, celery, carrot, red grape, beet prune, apricot and strawberry
Bronchitis	:	Spinach, tomato, onion, carrot, apricot, pineapple, lemon and peach
Bladder ailments	:	Watercress, parsley, apple, lemon, apricot, carrot, cucumber and celery

Colds	:	Spinach, onion, celery, carrot, grapefruit, pineapple, orange, lemon
Colitis	:	Apple, pineapple, apricot, peach, pear, spinach, cucumber, beet, carrot and papaya
Constipation	:	Watercress, spinach, beet, lemon, carrot, appeal, pear and grapes
Diarrhoea	:	Celery, carrot, lemon, pineapple, papaya
Diabetes	:	Spinach, lettuce, carrot, celery, citrus fruits
Epilepsy	:	Carrot, celery, red grapes and spinach
Eczema	:	Red grapes, cucumber, beet, carrot, and spinach
Eye disorders	:	Spinach, apricot, carrot, parsley, celery and tomato
Gout	:	Spinach, celery, carrot, tomato, cucumber, red sour cherries, beet and pineapple
Heart disease	:	Red grapes, spinach, carrot, lemon, beet and cucumber
Headache	:	Grapes, spinach, carrot, lettuce and lemon
Halitosis	:	Apple, spinach, pineapple, grapefruit, tomato, carrot, lemon and celery
High blood pressure	:	Beet, carrot, orange, grapes and cucumber

Insomnia	: Celery, grapes, apple, lettuce, lemon and carrot
Influenza	: Orange, spinach, pineapple, onion, grapefruit, carrot, orange and apricot
Jaundice	: Celery, grapes, carrot, pear, beet, spinach, lemon and cucumber
Kidney disorders	: Lemon, carrot, parsley, apple, cucumber, orange and celery
Liver ailments	: Cucumber, papaya, carrot, lemon, tomato, beet and grapes
Menopausal symptoms	: Seasonal vegetables and fruits
Menstrual disorders	: Beet, grapes, cherry, lettuce, prunes, spinach and turnips
Neuritis	: Apple, orange, pineapple, beet and carrot
Obesity	: Carrot, lettuce, beet, papaya, cherry, grapefruit, lemon, orange, pineapple, tomato, cabbage and spinach
Psoriasis	: Cucumber, beet, grapes and carrot
Prostate problems	: Carrot, asparagus, spinach, lettuce and all fruit juice in season
Piles	: Watercress, spinach, pineapple, orange, lemon, papaya, carrot and turnip

Rheumatism	:	Spinach, beet, grapefruit, orange, grapes, lemon, tomato, cucumber and carrot
Stomach ulcers	:	Carrot, grapes, apricot and cabbage
Sore throat	:	Parsley, tomato, pineapple, grapes, apricot, lemon, prune and carrot
Sinus problems	:	Radish, carrot, lemon, apricot, tomato and onion
Tonsillitis	:	Spinach, carrot, pineapple, grapefruit, lemon, apricot, orange and radish.
Varicose veins	:	Watercress, orange, carrot, plum, beetroot, tomato and grapes.

As some of the above fruits and vegetables are seasonal, I have given a wide variety of fruits and vegetables to choose from. Taking fruits and vegetables, while ignoring a normal diet is not going to harm your health in any way whatsoever, therefore, you can always try to make use of these natural therapies. The idea is not to discourage you from taking medicine, which you may be taking for many years for heart and blood pressure.

Lastly, a reminder – avoid self-medication except in case of emergencies like take a tablet of sorbitrate when the blood pressure is very high otherwise even long-term medicines should be taken under medical guidance.

An annual health check-up is also a good idea. Get a complete body check-up done which will include lungs, liver and kidney function test, total heart check-up including trade-mill, colour doppler, etc. Do not forget to list out the problems you may be facing at the time of health check-up, so that they send you to the concerned specialist.

I would like to conclude this long section on health management with the golden words: "There is no substitute for exercise and diet control to maintain good health."

Ageing is a natural process

He who is calm and happy in nature will hardly feel the pressure of age, but to him who is of an opposite disposition – youth and age are equally a burden. We all know the phases of life starting from childhood, it's quite natural to grow age-wise and this process of ageing cannot be stopped.

Recently, a research study was conducted in USA where it was found that aging can be predicted from the bones of a person because the speed of physical aging is strongly influenced by genetics. A biological marker was also developed to represent the age of the bones of the body. Scientist Leonid Kalichman from Boston University was one of the researchers for this study. According to him the marker can be used by doctors as a scientific tool for predicting a person's general functioning and life span. If a doctor can determine that a person is ageing faster than the normal then measures such as vitamin supplements and exercises should be recommended so as to help in slowing down the process. He further emphasised and classified the markers as grey hair, wrinkles or skin elasticity to estimate biological age. These features are hard to quantify. If the finding of this study can be workable then a person at the age of 90 may be able to function as if he was 30. It is felt that biological ageing will be a hot topic of study in the coming years especially in the West, where people are living longer than ever before.

The above study is based on the investigation of the bones of about 400 Russian families comprising 787 men within the age group 18-89 years and 723 women in the age group of 18-90. The results indicated that men and women inherit different ageing patterns because in men the genes expressed are more likely to influence how quickly they will age whereas in women the genes are more likely to represent at what age visible changes in the bone will begin to appear. We hope that the result of this new study will join a battery of other tools used by scientists who research again to have ways to fight it. At the end of the day the quest of scientists and doctors is to help people function better than their chronological age, that is the age written on their passports.

We Indians are not behind, rather we are ahead of the world. Look at the techniques of yoga, exercises, meditation, diet management; they all go for age reversal process that is why you will find a number of yogis over 90 years of age still working as if they are just over 40. I may quote the example of my own uncle Air Marshal S.N. Goyal who is 92 years of age. He was a fighter pilot of Royal Air Force commissioned by king George personally. He is the man who introduced yoga for defence cadets when he was commending national defence academy. When you ask the secret of his health, he may not say what it is, but we all know that it is yoga and strict diet control. He travelled abroad and taught yoga in more than 15 countries of the world and preached age reversal.

Sex is important if not essential

When I am addressing this issue to people who are 50 years or more then I must be careful because sex is still a taboo subject among the people of this generation. Sex is equated by the people nearing the age of retirement with character. What happens when you are 50 and your better half is still in the 40s, the frequency of having sex reduces to a great extent. You make an excuse that the wife is undergoing menopause giving a false satisfaction to the myth that she does not require sex or does not feel the urge for it. This is not true. As a man you still feel quite active and energetic when it comes to sex. You may fantasize having sex with the women you like because our culture, our values and the concept of sex associated with character do not allow us to have multiple partners. Another reason is your trust, understanding and bonding with your wife. You feel that the same standards should apply for husband and wife. When you cannot allow your wife to enjoy sex with others then what way you can have this right. Your life partner may not be experiencing orgasm during sex as an Indian women she is too inhibited to complain. She may feel the urge for sex but will not voice it out openly. You being a male may satisfy your sexual urge by seeing pornographic films, fantasizing and masturbating. Just think how many time you were with your wife both physically and mentally while having sex. Can you be true to your conscious that you achieved satisfaction by way of dreaming or fantasizing about an imaginary woman or someone other than your partner. I do not have anything against people adopting this kind of practices, it is their personal affair which nobody has got a right to moralize about.

Man remains active sexually for a longer period of time to a woman, if we talk in terms of fertility. Men even at the age of 90, can have sufficient sperm count in their semen for fathering a child. You may ask why all this discussion over the matter of sex? Why do we need sexual satisfaction? Yes, let me say, sex can be a cure for many ailments. Look at the people who are enjoying a healthy sex life because for them sex is not only pleasurable but gives substantial health benefits, both physical and psychological.

Headache can be cured by sex

Do you enjoy sex with body or mind? The answer will come–the mind only. Nearing the age of retirement you avoid sex with the excuse of headache, but, let's understand that one of the health benefits of sex is the ability to act as a pain reliever, because the hormone oxytocin is released in your body whenever you engage in sexual activity. Another hormone like chemical endorphins, is also released which is somewhat like morphine. It is scientifically proven that when a person is aroused, his oxytocin level begins to rise till orgasms finally and release the pain of all kinds whether it be headaches, cramps, or overall body aches. Again, I would like to emphasise that age is the factor.

Stress is reduced

You will observe the people who are not having enjoyable sex life suffer from tension, depression, frustration and look irritable. Most of the time it manifests as short-tempered behaviour. Sex can be a remedy for overcoming stress. Many a times you find that after having orgasm the man usually fall asleep when it is the time to liberate in true sense both self and partner. Many people enjoy a regular dose of sex and they sleep much better at night, feel alive and refreshed throughout the day. Another benefit of sex is good sleep allowing you to handle day-to-day stress in an efficient manner.

Blood flow boosts by sex

It is of common knowledge that when you get aroused your blood starts to pump at a quicker rate and it is quite natural that the blood flow to the brain increases. The increased heart-rate and blood volume to the brain result in better performance in and out of bed. The fresh supply of blood pumping through the body provides a healthy dose of oxygen to organs. We can say that sex is a cleaning agent for the body system. Otherwise also, look at the various postures shown in the *Kamasutra* which advocates best kind of exercises with sexual pleasure. Enjoying in *Kamasutra* way is only possible when you are keeping a flexible body by way of regular exercise and yoga.

A final word on sex

Let's debate on situations where you find yourself in a dilemma. Let's take a situation when your wife is over 50 and you are nearing the age of retirement. You have observed that your sex life is nearly at the finishing end. You do feel the urge and dream about sexual pleasure but you hardly get an occasion. Because whether you accept it or not it is like taking the same food or vegetable throughout your life on a daily basis. I am not joking. We are bound by our values, traditions and definitions which make sex as routine and we cannot break it.

Recently, I met a friend, who is in his late 50s. He goes abroad quite often. When I asked about his sex life he says occasionally he sleeps with his wife but she has permitted him to enjoy sex with other women. When I asked what about his attitude towards his wife. Look at the male ego and dominance, he says I am ready to allow my wife to enjoy sex with others but she says that I could not find a better person in the world who can satisfy the way you can, you are my He man. My friend feels relaxed. I asked him have you ever enjoyed sex with other women? He answered – yes, before marriage it was a great fun, with a number of women. And now, with the permission of the wife here is the chance. Don't you agree that men are opportunists. They follow a philosophy which suits them.

Let's see where the new generation is going. Look at the government policies, imparting sex education at the secondary school level. Installing condom vending machines not only in the public places, but in universities. Recently, the Indian Railways have announced that they are going to install condom vending machines at all the railway stations. All this is going in the name of AIDS prevention.

In the north-east condoms are promoted with the excuse that a large number of army of soldiers is there. Just imagine, you are taking the care of soldier's sex life, but what will happen to the local women there? Will they be not the victim? Have we ever thought of legalizing prostitution which is the oldest profession in the world? Women are being victimized, exploited and harassed, for satisfying the sexual lust of men. Whether it is the police, pimps or anti-social elements they all are taking the advantage of laws relating to prohibition of prostitution.

Now, you are about to retire but you feel quite young, enjoy seeing photographs of beautiful girls in magazines or watching steamy videos or films. What solution I can give to you? Let's take something from the younger generation. Sex to them is not a taboo subject rather it is very open. I remember one of my secretaries having an affair with a boy, was always quite open in asking my permission to leave early for a date. One day I asked what is this date? She frankly said it is the day when she goes out with his boyfriend and have fun. Being a man from the old school of thought,I asked do you intend to marry this boy? She said, yes, of course! It was my question again, as to what will happen if, it does not happen for some reason? She replied, "No problem, I will find another partner. It's okay, we both enjoyed. I take sex as a game rather a good physical exercise."

The above instance is no longer shocking. The younger generation feels comfortable to eliminate sex while defining character. What is the moral of the story for you? If you lost your life partner, I feel you may have two options. First, devote your time and energies reading spiritual books becoming somewhat ascetic about sex. Second, prepare yourself mentally for changing the definition of character. Play safe by way of a live-in relationship or a second marriage or enjoy sex with someone but take precautions for AIDS, etc.

I know that the above discussion on the issue of sex may not be palatable for some of the readers. Therefore, I feel you may take it as an opinion only. As a matter of fact, I researched on the topic of managing stress and the suggestions are based on these findings. It will not be out of place to mention that my book titled *Living a Stressful Life with Joy*, addressing the issue of stress, is quite popular in India and abroad.

Spiritual Wisdom for Peace

Change has a considerable psychological impact on the human mind.
To the fearful it is threatening because it means that things may get worse.
To the hopeful it is encouraging because things may get better.
To the confident it is inspiring because the challenge exists to make things better.

Islam Ahmed is now 55 years of age and is in the process of planning for his retirement. He has no problem with regard to finances and house, etc. because being in a multinational company he is comfortable with good financial package. He has his own house and children are studying abroad. Islam Ahmed, being the youngest in the family, is facing emotional setbacks due to certain things which are natural and beyond control. Last year, he lost his father. He was not being able to come out from this trauma when his mother also expired just three months after. Though, the parents were old and died at the right age but Islam Ahmed was feeling as if, vital portion has been taken away from his body.

It was not only the loss of his parents which was creating a vacuum in his mind but he was feeling too much vacuum at emotional level for the loss of many other near relatives one after other. The news of passing away of his dear professors, distant relatives, was haunting him. It was only a month back when he lost his elder brother-in-law, who was over 75 years of age and died a natural death. Close friends and relatives tried to console Islam Ahmed about the natural process of death. But he was not being able to accept the true hard facts of life. While planning for retirement, he was feeling afraid of losing many more near and dear ones. At times he used to feel as if, it was a punishment to be the youngest in the family because he will have to witness these kinds of tragedies in the near future also.

When I am addressing the issue of spirituality, especially in the context of wisdom for peace, I feel amazed as to whether there can be any planning for having peace? Can we find solution for the problems of Islam Ahmed? Well, our religions are clear about the concept of life and death. If we talk about *Bhagvad Gita*, the message is very loud and clear. Even in Islam and Christianity the inherent meanings come the same and distinguish body and soul separately. When you are reaching the age of 60 then it is quite natural that your elders will be at the fag end of their life. I know that you cannot think about the death of your relatives. Nobody should. But there can be mental preparedness, we may say that what we meet in life is fixed, but how we meet is not fixed. Death has to happen. You can't help it, but how you will meet this loss and how you will react? It is all in your hands. Whether you take it as a ground reality of life by mourning day and night ignoring that there are others living with you and you are duty bound to keep them happy or you accept the things it is up to you.

You must understand and accept that your mother and father can't be so dear to anybody else from your in-laws side, may be your wife and for that matter your children too, because the number of years you have spent with them and the bonding due to blood relation can't be equated by others.

When you hear the sad news of the demise of your in-laws you will realize that the pain is different and you are feeling more sad about your wife so try to console her. It is easy to talk on this issue but it is difficult to practise the concept of life and death. I feel when you plan for retirement. It is not the same planning what you have done at the beginning of your career. Because you have lived your life, you have seen the world in your own way.

Nobody wants to die, even a person suffering with multiple ailments, struggling for life in the hospital still keeps a hope to survive. Mercy killing is not lawful. We feel so much attached with the body that a person is allowed to be on ventilator while in coma for months together with a hope that one day he will come out of it. I feel a healthy body with a working life can only give meaning that you are living in this world. That is why so much emphasis is given on health planning.

Giving a different meaning to life

Let us presume and believe in the concept that we never die. Here the meaning of 'we' is the spirit or the soul, which resides in our body. The body is just like a costume which has been at work for years and a day comes when we feel like changing it, mainly because it is torn, faded and shattered.

A question comes in my mind while writing on this issue, as to whether there is a need to change our lifestyle in old age or one can continue in the same way. Look at the lifestyle of industrialists, artists, writers, advocates, doctors, etc. who do not feel the necessity of changing the lifestyle. For them life continues as before. But the percentage of such people is quite low. Generally when we grow old, especially in the Indian context, our values, culture and religious feelings compel us towards spirituality. There are a number of factors which influence a person in old age. The status of a grandparent, poor health, and loss in earning capacity with free available time add to the desire for peace with emotional stability which derives us towards spiritualism.

It is not easy to define spirituality because over a period of time its meaning has enlarged to a great extent. In today's world even management is having the concept of spirituality. Human relations have bypassed other aspects which are of technical nature because there is a man behind the machine and the man whosoever he may be, is having a heart and mind to feel. It is the sensitivity level and emotional hunger which requires motivation to do any task.

Love – the essence of life

Before the issue is discussed for its deep meanings let us start with the word with the four alphabet - LOVE. You all know what is love? But I am certain that the concept and meaning of love are different in your mind. Love is the most natural feeling for every living being which has been given by God. The love is not confined to human beings it is known and practised by animals also. Well, you are nearing the age of retirement and purpose of writing all this to assist you to plan for it better. But I am compelled to talk on love. If you have not experienced this wonderful feeling earlier let me say that you must have not one but three love in your life.

Let's start with the **first love**. It is the love for yourself. You should love yourself the most by attributing all adjectives and superlative qualities attributed to yourself. A woman at any age may feel that she is the most intelligent and beautiful woman in this world. Similarly, a man must feel that he is the most handsome and brilliant in the world. There is no comparable to your personality. You are fascinated and try to fall madly in love with yourself. Stand before a full size mirror and say to yourself "I Love You". If there is any problem you are facing just talk to yourself and say boldly "I will overcome it by winning". I have the courage, strength, and conviction to fight the troubles. Have confidence in yourself that you will succeed. You will find that your conversation with your image is a good question-answer session as if you are conversing with your conscious. When you are in love it is natural that the questions and answers will be positive because you think only good about the person you love. This first love becomes necessary in old age because now you perhaps have lot of psychological and emotional problems to worry about. Don't confine this practice of love to yourself. Share it with your spouse so that he or she may also practice it. In old age only your spouse can empathize with. You will find that your love for your spouse is growing with each passing year because of sharing and caring.

Now comes the **second love**. This love is also very important because here you love the job you are doing. Some people may say that they have no job to do after retirement. But still they have some job because an empty mind is a devil's workshop. Whether you are reading in your spare time, cooking, gardening, singing or exercising or having a normal job or business, all these activities come under second love. You need to love these jobs otherwise you will not enjoy doing them. Sometimes you get a job which you don't like but still you need to love it. So force yourself to love it. The second love will give you happiness and peace of mind. While performing a particular task, say "I love it". Try to develop a sentimental and emotional attainment with your job. Again, say it as if you are talking to yourself "this is my job, I love it, nothing is impossible, I can do it". These affirmations will increase your energy to perform the task at hand in an effective manner.

Now, it is the turn for your **third love**, which is also as important as the first two loves. This is the love which you all know – it is the love for your spouse, relatives and friends and associates. You can't live if this third love is not present, because at times your need a shoulder to rest your tiring head. You feel like having somebody who can wipe out your tears. A person who can share your feelings by asking the question "why are you sad?" This love is much above empathy. Because it is coming from the person who knows you, your likes and dislikes, your concept of happiness and sorrow, your emotional and sensitivity level and above all you as a person with all your pluses and minuses. This love from the people and your love for the people will be there because they have accepted you with all your strengths and weaknesses. You love your children and parents because these are blood relations. In some isolated cases there is hatred among relatives but ultimately during testing times it is family and the love embedded in it which prevails.

Love for everybody

Somebody asked me as to which love is most important, if one has to practise all the above three loves. I think there is no need of prioritizing any of these three loves, because they complement each other. You cannot say that the first love is less important or the third love is more important. When you are growing old sometimes when you go down the memory lane and suddenly you recall few people who you considered as enemies. If you are active after retirement you may find your enemies are still there. Who are your enemies? In fact they are the persons who are jealous of you and hate you for the reasons you may or may not be knowing. How to come out from the situation of having enemies, which is no doubt disturbing. Why not apply the third love to them? You may not agree with me because your enemies cannot be a relative or friend, then how to love them? Do not worry, I will give you sufficient reasons and justification for loving your enemies. Just think that, your relatives or the people of your third love remember you only in the case of happiness or sorrow, when you are in trouble they remember you and come to your aid and when you are happy they will associate in your happiness. There will be few such occasions, it will not be an everyday affair. But look at your enemy. He remembers you day and night, thinks about you, while eating, sleeping, walking, even while at work. You are always in their mind. Now, tell me who can be dearer than an enemy who remembers you day and night, thinking about you, planning against you, try to find out where you are, what you are doing. So much energy is invested on you at the cost of his own happiness, because planning against you also gives tension to him. Don't you feel you need to love your enemy? It should be natural to love your enemy, who feels so much concerned about you all the time more than your near and dear. Believe me; loving an enemy will give you peace of mind.

Teachings from religion

Our thoughts and feelings form a part of our personality. They are inter-related like flower and fragrance. If you lack profound feelings then your thoughts will become weak and ineffective. Similarly, if your thoughts are ego-centric and negative then the feelings of the heart will become like a polluted stream with anger, pride, hate and other impurities. Wrong ways of thinking and feeling make you to acquire certain weaknesses which do not allow the development of your inner potentiality. But these are all temporary phases like clouds in the sky obscuring the brilliance of the sun. Our soul is essentially divine which is pure, however, there are six dangerous enemies which affect its purity. These are–

- Desire for sense pleasures in general, passion in particular
- Anger
- Greed for money, lavishness and other pleasures
- Delusion coming in the form of infatuation
- Pride
- Jealousy, for not being able to tolerate others' pride.

The above impurities which can also be termed as vices are inter-related. They actually include all negative qualities that effect human personality. These are your enemies right from your childhood. When you are reaching old age the need for conquering these enemies becomes essential, otherwise, you cannot enjoy real prosperity and peace in life. Once you overcome these vices you may attain enlightenment. It should be a challenge before you and you must consider these vices as weaknesses and endeavour to remove them so that you attain spiritual fulfillment.

Let's take the ancient view from Vedic literature which throws some light on the above enemies of the soul. There is a quotation in *Atharvaveda* (8/4/22) and *Rigveda* (7/6/104), which says;

"O Indra, may you crush by your thunderbolt the demon that moves in the form of an owl, an owl's young one, a dog, a chakravaka or ruddy goose, an eagle, and a vulture."

If we go, try and understand the meanings of the above quote the question will come as to what is demon in the form of an owl, is it infatuation or delusion? We all know that owls cannot see during the day. Therefore, we can easily understand that owl is a symbol of a person who is blinded by delusion. Such a person can see only within the range of his egoistic feelings but beyond that he is like a blind man. The other question is who is the demon in the form of an owl's young one? Is it jealousy which thrives in the absence of the light of rationality and reasoning? If you want to understand other people's life, you will observe that there is nothing to be jealous about because everybody has some shortcomings or the other.

You can understand that being jealous of someone's prosperity is totally irrational. It comes because of blind vision like a owl. Now let us see what is the demon which comes in the form of a dog. It is anger. When dogs fight they are totally unable to control themselves. You may teach your dog all kinds of lessons but when another dog challenges him he loses his temper completely. Another demon that comes is in the form of desire for self pleasures and passion and can be understood as an animal who is well known for his enormous courtship, and the demon that soars in the form of an eagle is egoistical pride. Lastly, the demon in the form of vulture is greed. If your are seized with greed, you lose your sense of discrimination, just like a vulture which eats all types of rubbish without any reservations.

Indra in the above context is God, the Almighty. As an aspirant you seek the blessing of God for destruction of all the enemies of the soul. Now, think as to whether for your own shortcomings you will allow yourself in a position of an uncontrolled angry dog and Indiscriminating vulture. Unfortunately, wrong ways of thinking and feeling often makes you less virtuous rather than more elevated. You cannot overcome these shortcomings when you are in the clutches of these enemies. You cannot overcome the situation when you are in the clutches of these enemies. The only requirement is to have consistent introspection. Believe me, at any age of your life you can become the embodiment of divine bliss and perfection.

You need to win over vices

The question comes as to how one can win over the above six vices. There are three kinds of people: the one who learns from the mistakes of others - respects him for he is a wise man; the second is one who learns from his own mistakes - he is a smart person, follow him; the third category of person is he who observes the mistakes being committed but do not learn anything - ignore him. We all agree that these six vices one way or the other come in the way of achieving wisdom or peace. I am not suggesting that all these vices are there in you. Just think, even a single vice can affect your peace of mind.

Desire – a natural weakness

When we think about the sense of pleasure, in general, and passion, in particular, the desire for it comes automatically. It has got a number of meanings because desire may include values such as ethical, material, vital and spiritual. Basically, desire signifies establishment of a joyous relationship with family members, friends and those around you. The relationship should be meaningful. It may be for material wealth or ethical values of life. It may be for moving towards liberation, as you feel in old age.

We generally talk about desire as impurity of mind, which is opposed to the ethical values of life, whereas in reality, desire is essential in life. But if your desires are not within limits, then your mind will be infested with unfulfilled desires which will not allow you to be in peace.

As a matter of fact, desires are like a net in which human conscience, if trapped, the bird of human soul wishes to fly away in the regions of freedom but is caught in the net of desires. It suffers untold misery. A person seeking peace, prosperity, self-realization and immortality must learn the art of studying and purifying his desires. Otherwise, unfulfilled and frustrated desires will lead to tension locking the will power. The desires can be unconscious or conscious.

Some stories based on real life situations teach us the lesson with lasting impression. That desire is our greatest enemy. This is what we can understand from this story.

There was a blacksmith who used to labour very hard but still enjoyed his work immensely, and sang songs joyfully while working. The blacksmith had a rich neighbour who used to hear him singing and feel extremely jealous. The rich man wondered as to how it could be that with so much of hard labour this poor blacksmith was always feeling happy. Whereas he with all the wealth was not being able to sleep at night due to anxiety and worries.

One day the rich man secretly threw a bag containing 99 thousand rupees in the shop of the blacksmith. When next day the blacksmith opened his shop he found the bag and wondered how it had come in his shop. He decided to keep the money and make good use of it. Then an idea came to his mind that it is only 99 thousand rupees, why not earn more money to make it one lakh rupees. The coming days he worked so hard that he earned 5 thousand rupees. Now he had 1 lac 4 thousand rupees, the blacksmith thought this figure is quite odd and that he should earn Rs. 1 thousand more to make it a better figure. He laboured very hard to earn more money. In return his earning again was 4 thousand making a total of Rs.1 lakh 8 thousand. It never gave satisfaction to him because the figure was still odd. So the next day he worked even harder and this pattern continued with him always needing a little more to make a nice round figure.

The days passed like this for him earning more and more money. He lost the peace and joy with which he used to work. Now there were no more songs on his lips. The rich man was delighted because he had succeeded in his plan. One day the blacksmith realised that he was becoming weak, sick and restless. He thought of his earlier days of happiness. It came to his mind that all this trouble has started with that 99 thousand rupees. The moment he felt convinced about the root cause of the problem, he felt a great sense of relief. Now, it was his turn to gather the entire money and threw it over to the rich man's place thinking that the rich man would be able to make better use of this enormous wealth.

The moral of the story is that we should not be entangled by 99 because the moment you get caught by the illusion of needing more of something to be happy you become entangled like the blacksmith in a joyless situation. The desires for things which are perishable are full of vanity; therefore, we should desire for only self-realization and development of spiritual values and virtues. Finally, we must desire to become desireless. Every religion speaks about the importance of overcoming lustful passion; even the management theories advocate this concept. It says man is a wanting animal, if one desire is satisfied another arises and this process goes on from birth till death.

Look at the inner beauty of your spouse

I am not here to debate on the issue of love and arranged marriages, their merits and demerits. My idea is to highlight the importance of loving your partner more and more as you grow older. Normally, it so happens that during your courtship days your love is at its peak. You start appreciating everything about all actions of your would-be partner, may be the hairs, smile, eyes. But after marriage over a period of time it takes declining trend. However, in arranged marriages, initially you do not love your life partner because you do not know the person, it is the beginning of love knowing each other slowly with the passage of time. In most of the cases the love grows. There is an interesting story which speaks about inner love and gives the massage that true love sees the inner beauty.

There was a prince who considered himself very sensuous and handsome. One day while walking in the garden he saw a peasant girl who was extremely beautiful. The prince was enchanted by her beauty. He immediately proposed to her and told her that he was willing to marry her right away to make her the princess. The young girl was already in love with somebody. She was stunned with the proposal and got confused as to how to refuse the prince. She knew that it was not possible to make the prince angry by refusal because then she would be forced to marry him. Suddenly an idea struck to her mind and she requested the prince for little time before her yes. The prince agreed and told her to come the next day. The prince was dreaming of returning the next day to claim his bride. Soon after the prince departed, the clever young lady swallowed a powerful herb which made her ugly looking and deformed.

Next day, when the prince came he could not find the beautiful young woman instead he found a sad looking ugly woman. The prince could not afford to bear her horrible looks. He asked her, "Where is the beautiful girl I saw yesterday?" The lady replied, "Prince I am the same girl who is to be your bride, I accepted your proposal. The only thing is that I am not feeling well right now." The prince was horrified and hurriedly left.

The above story has got a great moral teaching. The prince could see only the external form of the woman and not the beauty of her spirit. Similarly, we can see that romantic love is confined to the externalities of a person and is incredibly selfish. I feel you all should think and realize that when you are drawn in a love relationship you must ask yourself, "If my partner grows old losing the beauty and charm of youth or marred by illness or accident, will I continue to love with the same intensity?" Look at your answer coming from your conscience, if it is no, then your love is nearly a free violity, because a meaningful love demands understanding, sacrifice and passion. Now, you are nearing the age of retirement, your relationship should mutually assist one another to rise the higher levels of understanding and awareness.

Anger–relates to temperament

I think it is one of the most commonly used words to describe the personality of a person. Anger has many degrees ranging from ordinary annoyance to an intense violent rage, contempt, intolerance, vengeance, and hatred. All these words are related forms of anger. One should not be afraid of this 'vice' because even the highly educated and apparently religious people suffer from this malady. Anger is accompanied by hatred and revenge, quite common in society. However, when we think about enjoying the spiritual values of life it is necessary to remove this terrible vice. Anger has got a number of negative side effects, which comes in the form of creating illusions, wastage of mental energy, promoting chaos and dissipating will power.

Though anger as a vice is not necessarily an evil without reason. Sometimes it is rational because of being hurt by someone or as the result of having been inflicted by physical or psychological injury. A person suffering from this kind of behaviour enters into a state of anger in a natural way. But there are situations when people become angry and hateful for no reason at all, may be due to irrational functioning of their intellect. It is the part of the personality which stems from psychological impressions gathered in childhood. Deep seated anger are impressions of dislike in the unconscious mind which causes agitation. There are people who justify their outbursts of anger as righteous indignation. Some people call it a terminology which was applied to 'Jesus' for a display of anger in a temple when he saw that things are not being done in proper manner. He threw everything around to show his displeasure. Similarly, Krishna and Arjuna also displayed righteous anger in 'Mahabharat War'.

Now it is your turn to think about your anger. In the past as parents you too had many a moments. You may recall that it was necessary to discipline your children and your cool and calm behaviour would not have worked. This type of anger is of a special nature which has got a proper place in life. I am not here to negate the existence of anger in absolute terms because some angers are there for spiritual purpose. It will be appropriate to call it "love backed anger". Please do not get confused to justify every anger as righteous indignation because these are very few. Their real test of anger is to see if it is truly purposeful because in that case it will not deeply agitate your mind. It will not disturb your reason, you will not lose your power of observation and balance. Let me simplify the righteous anger by calling it knife by a skillful chef. Because it is there to cut vegetables and not your fingers.

Anger results in mindless action

The feeling of anger begins in our heart and it affects not only the family but all our relationships. It is like a fire which sparks and spreads. How does it happen? There is a good example of a scene which was created in a honey vendor's shop. A honey vendor was selling honey in his shop. While doing so a drop of honey fell on the ground without the knowledge of the people there. A lizard spotted the honey and started licking it. The shopkeeper's cat saw the lizard and immediately pounced on it. In the meantime, a dog entered the shop and seeing the cat got excited. The dog attacked and injured the cat. The shopkeeper witnessing this scene got very angry and grabbed a stick to beat the dog, with the result that dog's leg was broken. The owner of the dog got infuriated and started beating the shopkeeper. The other shopkeepers came down and could see that a customer was beating the honey vendor. They tried to save the honey vendor. The customer also shouted for help and some of his friends in the crowd came to his rescue. Within a short span of time the crowd increased because whosoever heard the fight going on started gathering there to enquire what was going on. Now it was a fight free for all. Nobody knew for whom they were fighting – the shopkeeper or the customer. It was a tremendous fight which resulted in ruining of the shop since the entire honey stored in the shop was spilled over. Now look at the moral of this story. Visualise anger as the spilled drops of honey. I think now you can understand about the ramifications of anger which can disturb a harmonious atmosphere by creating tension and discord, hurting others as well as yourself.

Now the question comes how to control anger? Anger expresses in three ways; physical, verbal and mental. When an uncultured person becomes angry he can hit the person who has provoked him. This anger is to be controlled in such a manner that the effect is reduced by way of uttering harsh words rather than physical expression of it causing injury and damage. The second step in controlling anger is to curtail verbal expression when you need to strive to control your speech and harbour the anger in your mind. This will save you from painful repercussion of uttering harsh words. This control is necessary irrespective of the justification that your anger was rational because an uncontrolled tongue always leads to regret, repentance and wastage of energy.

You may recall in *Mahabharat* when Yudhisthira asks Bhishma, "What is one great quality that can enable a person to be successful anywhere in the world in all projects?" Bhishma replies, "Mastery over the tongue, if you could stop expressing anger through your tongue your success would be secured in all directions."

How to win over anger

It is well said that God gave us two ears but only one tongue which is a gentle hint that we should listen more and talk less. Let us remember to keep our mind in gear before putting our tongue into action. Finally, our ultimate goal is to eliminate ill-will from our minds and set ourselves free from afflictions of mental anger. Whenever, we harbour anger in our mind somewhere we hurt ourselves and sometimes we are not even aware of the evil done by us. Your anger is directed towards a person and it will affect him only when he is vulnerable otherwise your anger will simply boomerang on you and will hurt you. Just think if you wish somebody to go to hell then you yourself will be going there to visualize as to how that man will actually suffer in hell. Out of anger we curse each other, but in reality we are cursing ourselves.

Life is short and we must utilize it for higher purposes. We should not allow our mind to acquire the habit of being angry over trifling things. We need to introspect by looking within ourselves now and then. If you are creating dissension and tension during the first half of the day, believe me the rest of the day will be spent just worrying about the repercussion. It will not end here, the next day you will struggle to remedy the situation. Just think about the time and energy you have wasted.

Let us conserve our energy for attaining self-realization by practising endurance, patience, forgiveness and generosity of mind as far as possible. You may ask a question as to how is it possible not to show anger when it is rational and reasonable or on provocation? The answer lies in your own self-realization that the evil doer and provocateur is a sick person. If a doctor is caring for a sick patient how he will deal with that person if the patient is throwing things around. Then it is natural that the doctor will try to save himself from injury. But the doctor will never start throwing things back in anger towards the patient. You must behave like the doctor as he will wait for an opportunity to help the patient. It is a piece of advice that we should have that type of attitude in dealing with all those who seek to harm us. You cannot win over anger by anger.

Looking anger as a slave

Just think if your teeth bite your tongue will you knock them off. You would never think of knocking your teeth because both teeth and tongue are important. You take care of your teeth by going to the dentist. Similarly, we are related to all the people around us just as our teeth are related to our tongue, or our hand is related to our feet.

You must have heard of the name of Alexander the Great, whose guru was a devotee of Indian philosophy. One day the guru told Alexander, if you go to India you must try to conquer the kingdom but if you honour my advice it will be of far greater importance to visit a sage and try to bring him along with you. Alexander listened to the advice of his guru and on reaching India he followed the guru's advice by visiting a well-known sage. He gave his introduction the same way the people knew him as Alexander the Great, a conqueror, an emperor. Alexander was amazed to see the saint did not say anything nor bowed his head before him. Alexander could not control his anger at the behaviour of sage and asked him that didn't he know that he had conquered half of the world and no one was greater than him. How is it that he did not give respect to him? The sage remained calm and replied patiently, "Because you are the slave of my slave." Alexander became even more angry and shouted, "What do you mean? I can cut you down with a sword." The sage laughed. Do you think I am this body that you can cut down? Alexander became quite and asked for further explanation of the wise man's words. The saint replied "Alexander, you must know that anger, hate and greed are the greatest enemies and they are my slaves and by seeing your behaviour, I can understand that you are their slave. That is why you are the slave of my slaves."

Greed – with no limits

Desire and anger follows with this third vice which is enemy to peace and spirituality. The vice of greed has no limits. You are insecure unless you understand the negative aspect of this enemy. Greed is quite common all through your life. Sometimes it is embedded in your nature and you suffer this vice with no end to it. The greed may be for money, lavishness or any other worldly pleasure.

Let me narrate one story which is quite appropriate for understanding greed. In Tibet there is a temple with statue of thousands of Buddhas. Large numbers of devotees come there every day for worship. A devotee once selected one of the many Buddhas for his worship. To please the god everyday he used to bring costly incense and oil filled lamp with flowers to be placed before his chosen Buddha. But he was bemused that the fragrance of his incense used to drift towards other statutes Buddha of since he felt bad that the fragrance meant for his Buddha statue is going to other Buddha statue. He was quite frustrated and suddenly an idea came to his mind to prevent the fragrance from going to other Buddha statues. He went to a carpenter and created a wooden wall around his Buddha. Now he was happy to see that after placing this wooden wall, candle and incense fragment he kept before his Buddha statue confined to this space and the fragrance was confined in the box. After a week he was shocked to find that his Buddha became black due to the smoke. It had lost its lustre.

The morale of the story is that if you are the kind of a person who wants all happiness in life for yourself and none for others you are like this devotee who was striving not to let any fragrance go to any other Buddha statue. Walling yourself with I, me and mine attitude restricts your soul, limits your happiness. The Buddha or the spirit would become sooty with selfishness as a result when you look within yourself you will find more sorrow than happiness. Now see the reverse reaction. If you adopt a process of activity which opens your heart and freezes the soul instead of restricting it within yourself, I am sure you will observe that the Buddha within your heart shines in bright manner and you start to glow with joy.

The urge for pleasures is endless

You may be in your 50s or 60s but if, I ask you "Are you ageing or you have become old," certainly you will be hesitant to accept the fact. Ageing is natural process and one should not be afraid of it. But your feelings, your thoughts, your emotions and craving do not age. They do not decay though we ourselves continue to age. But side by side our craving appears to become more and more youthful.

You may recall the story of an ageing king. The king lived a lavish life enjoying the youthfulness all along for decades. A stage came when he noticed that he was ageing to enjoy the sensuous pleasures of life. He got so much worried with the thought that in the coming years he will not be able to enjoy the pleasures of life. The king got the blessings of a sage who gave him a boon with the power to exchange his age with any younger person willing to do so. The king asked his young children if any one of them would exchange their youth with his failing age. His elder son agreed to the proposal of exchanging his youth for the age of the king. The power of the boon worked and the king became young again and started living youth life with intense pleasures. Time never waits for anyone. The king again found his body ageing but still his craving for pleasure remained strong as ever. He realized the impossibility of ever satisfying worldly desires by merely having more and more experience. Finally a stage of self-realization came when he found himself filled with dispassion. The king wrote the following lines:

"Craving is like fire, and enjoyments of the senses are like oblations of clarified butter poured into the fire, making it blaze higher and higher. Who could ever quench fire by feeding its flame? The urge for pleasure cannot be fulfilled by all the pleasures of world."

This story conveys the meaning that one who peruses a quantitative concept of pleasure in life will never feels satisfied. He will simply continue to hanker for more and more which will never be fulfilled. Greed is just like a wolf, perhaps even hungrier than a wolf because a wolf has a limited hunger but greed has no limitation. If you are suffering from the vice of greed and you are not in a position to overcome the attachment of greed you must know that you are not aware of your own resources. You are only aware of what others have. The grass on the other side always look greener. You keep on thinking that others are better off than you. This condition is like a greedy dog. A dog sees food in front of other dog and thinks that food is much better than his, as a result he goes on barking instead of enjoying the food he had.

You must be thinking why I am taking the shelter of old stories in explaining the concept of vices. The sole idea is to reflect various aspects of vices by illustrating as to how it comes into existence.

Everybody wants to become rich. How much money? You can't limit it. There was a man who worshiped very hard. One day the deity came before him and offered him a boon that whatever he wished will be fulfilled. The man became very happy. The deity said everything you ask will be given to you but in addition to this all your neighbours in one block radius from your home will get double of whatever you get. At the first instance the man got confused and could not understand the implication of the deity's words, but he was quite pleased with this good fortune. He came back home and wished for a palatial house, immediately, his house was converted into a magnificent bungalow. But when he looked outside the window he found that his neighbours got a double storey palatial house. He then wished for a beautiful garden around his house. His wish was granted but the neighbours got flourishing garden twice the size of his garden. The man realized that his neighbours got double prosperity as compared to him. The man's heart began to burn with jealousy because it happened every time he asked for something. Finally, he became so upset that he hatched a very strange and crooked plan. He wished for a well in front of his house. Naturally his neighbours got two wells. Then he said let me have only one eye. His idea was that by wishing to become blind in one eye all his neighbours will become blind in both eyes and will fall into the wells. However, to his surprise this boon was not granted by the deity rather to teach the greedy and jealous devotee a spiritual lesson he was left with one eye and a well. While the neighbours were not harmed and everything was flourishing around them.

The moral of the above story is that there is so much illusion involved in trying to secure happiness through wealth. A greedy person is always comparing himself to others. What he has gained and achieved is never enough for him. Remember, if you are a millionaire you will feel happy until you meet a billionaire. There are always people who will surpass you in some way or other, not only in wealth but with health, looks, power, name and fame. The human heart can always be discontented. Therefore, if you want to go away from the vice of greed "do not compare yourself with others". Everyone has been given the best situation by God for advancement in unique manner. Please bear in mind that what has been given to you no one else can possess in exactly the same way.

Considering the negative aspect of greed you must realize that the moment your greed is eliminated your mind will feel relaxed and you will develop an awareness in your spirit and realize that this world is not your final stay rather you are in transit. As a personality your existence is only for a short time.

Pride – two sides of the coin

Pride as such is not a bad word and you may feel then why is it being termed a vice? Because one must feel a certain pride in himself in order to succeed in life and also to handle practical realities effectively. One should feel proud of being born as a human or like I said earlier for having first love. There are some forms of pride which concern with egoism, vanity, arrogance, cruelty and selfishness. These are the pride which needs to be identified as vices. The influence of this pride is so dangerous that it intoxicates the mind making you feel as if you don't know who are you? What are your goal and your sense of right from wrong? When it comes to the question of having the right or wrong pride one needs to behave like a crow with unique creature because it possesses only one eye that rolls back and forth between two sockets, whether it is biologically true or not but the idea is to follow the concept of double consciousness to switch the vision. You should not allow negative pride to come in your behaviour. At one moment we may feel about the negative pride but immediately, like a crow, we are back to the world aware of practical reality practising positive pride on yourself. In case your unconscious mind has not been purified and the real aspiration has not been developed then in that case the possessions, power and glory–all will create a twisted intellect and if you are lacking purity and somehow attain great power then it will be like a swollen head where you will never be able to handle the power and will fall.

When you turn towards egoistic feelings such as selfishness, vanity and greed your intellect will become gradually twisted. You may not realize but actually it will be creating a basis for future sorrow. Humility is another quality which can be considered as a divine virtue. In the context of pride let us recall the sermon of Lord Jesus who on the mount extols the great virtue of humility pointing towards majestic power. Jesus said, "Blessed are the meek, for they shall inherit the earth." The meekness should not be confused with dullness of mind or with humiliation but the blessed meekness by Lord Jesus can be understood as the state of advance personality integration in which one is so profoundly in tune with cosmic will that he has no need to assert his ego. In fact, he is guided by the divine hand and carries out the will of God with total surrender. The highest state of meekness is reached when you are being able to totally cast your ego into the ocean of divine.

Beware of inflated ego

You must be pondering on how to become free from ego. Again I must say that ego is not a vice as long as it is not inflated. To some people ego is their identity. The relaxation of ego is achieved only when you are sleeping when it is set aside not by your choice but by biological process. When you are moving from normal to supernormal awareness you will find that ego is not the source of your inspiration and initiative. You will observe that in real sense you are different from your ego. The self-realization will teach you the lesson as to how you can set aside the inflated ego by your own choice through increasing intuitional understanding. It will not be wrong to say that it is an art to become free of ego. But this art is acquired through a persistence process of personality integration by which you bring renewed health to your body and to your conscious and unconscious mind. Again you must remember that in case you are physically healthy then only it will be possible for you to detach from the body and if you are mentally healthy then it will be possible for you to detach from the mind. If your unconscious mind is not pressured by impure desires then it is possible for you to go beyond your ego. You need to balance yourself by right action, devotion, meditation, reflection and of course with good association. You will find that it is the beginning to develop a harmonized personality. You will realize that relaxing the inflated ego is not a difficult task. A feeling will come in your mind as if your spirit is a bird flying through the newly opened window of a cage making the bird free to soar beyond all limitations.

In day-do-day life, you should not allow pride and egoism becoming prominent in your behaviour. You will find that you are feeling humbler than a blade of grass and yet stronger than a mountain. The feeling will come as if you are lesser than a little glowworm and yet more effulgent than the sun. Do not forget that flowers never advertise their fragrance; the sun doesn't need to proclaim its brightness by beating drums. The ocean has no need to sing the praises of its profundity. Similarly, the Himalayas have no need to brag about their lofty heights. You are a human being an aspirant who unfolds the fragrance of virtue unravels the luminosity of spiritual wisdom, experience of *profundity* of universal life. You are here to ascend the heights of super consciousness. Therefore, you do not need to indulge in the pride and its numerous expressions.

I feel that the above detailed account of pride will give you an insight into its positive and negative aspects and you will have enough food for thought to recognize the negatives in order to achieve peace of mind.

Delusion – leads to confusion

We shall discuss the vices one by one which hinder the way of spirituality and wisdom for peace. These vices somewhere are interrelated with anger. There arises delusion which results in loss of memory and from loss of memory one loses the function of pure reasoning. Finally loss of reasoning leads toward distraction. We have used the word delusion which signifies obscuring of reasoning. Delusion causes the unenlightened mind to perceive a world of multiplicity. When you are in a state of delusion your mind will ignore the reality of the things and a stage will come in the philosophical manner that you will not feel the existence of ocean but will be attached to its waves. I may be allowed to say that you will ignore the sky to become attached to little clouds. Delusion causes the mind to be caught up by apparent values of family and society resulting in a scenario where you will feel completely confined to those values and circumstances. As an individual you will view yourself dependent on the family or the friends as if your joy and happiness is a result of their being. To understand various aspects of delusion, I may narrate a story relating to a family of thieves.

There was a king who was travelling alone, carrying a huge amount of treasure consisting of ornaments, precious stones, etc. Three thieves came to know about it. They followed the king and robbed him. They tied up the king and dumped him in a dry well. One of the thieves felt remorse after the robbery and developed a feeling of compassion for the king. He waited for an opportunity when the other two thieves went away. The thief came to the dry well secretly and untied the king. He told the king to go out in the forest as a free man. The king was surprised by this act of the thief and offered him to come with him so that he may reward him with money. The thief politely said that he cannot afford to receive the award of saving the king because he belongs to the family of thieves and cannot have the access to the royal palace.

The three thieves are symbolic of qualities we possess. In a way the two thieves who had gone away signify the bad elements whereas the third one is the true soul. The first two thieves keep your mind tied up with delusion. Now it is for the third thief as a quality in you to dilute. If you want to come out from delusion you need to make this third thief strong. At times you might feel that happiness is coming from the objects of situation that are outside of you. It makes you to secure those objects leading to a state of dependency and bondage. This quality of true soul comes for your rescue giving enlightenment showing you the real path you understand that happiness comes from within yourself.

The delusion comes with the sense of 'mineness' or 'possessiveness'. You feel so much attached with your friends and relatives that your mind says this life is nothing without them. You start forgetting the second love and this third love overpowers the first love. You are ageing now, you have seen the world. Your children have grown up. They have their own priorities. They can't have so much delusion with you now. But is it required? Just think whether you want to be a free bird or you want to live in the cage with all comforts losing the freedom to fly. Your family, friends and material possessions make you think in the natural way they are only things of importance and you live with these perishable things not realizing that your are essentially the spirit beyond time and space. The world of time and space is not your real and permanent home. Therefore you must live your life in such a way that world around you does not cripple your mind. Allow your mind to expand, breaking the delusions.

It is easy to talk about the ill effects of delusion but in old age it is really difficult to overcome, especially, when you see your grandchildren are playing with you. Though, it is difficult, let me tell you a fact of life. This world of delusion is like the ocean in which everyone is bobbing up and down, driven from one whirlpool to another. However, some people are there who surrender to the Almighty finding a ship to be taken on the right path towards life's destination, which is self-realization. When they reach even a more higher level there is a jet plane, and when they go to the higher levels–the sky–they get a rocket carrying them to a level beyond the gravitational force of earth. The delusion turns away from the divine soul.

There is another way of overcoming delusion, that is by joining some social activities, spending time with the organizations helping the poor and needy or with some people who are religious-minded ,may join the temple trust spreading the message of God. Yoga and meditation also help a lot in taking you away from delusion. Worshiping God, doing service to the humanity, fighting for a cause, to help the poor are the tools to win over delusion of your mind, which is making you attached to worldly things.

My idea is not to advise you to be away from your family and friends in the name of spirituality. The only objective for including this delusion as a vice is to make you understand to give priority to your own life and to your spouse. Don't feel so much attached with your relatives and friends that you feel totally dependent for their company.

Jealousy – a slow poison

Last but not the least, the sixth vice, jealousy is the most common vice. Jealousy is a form of vice where you are unable to tolerate others' pride. It has got many forms, mild to strong. The most common form of jealousy is when people perceive that someone else is surpassing them unfairly ranging from looks, popularity, wealth, happiness, fame and at times in spiritual advancement also. Jealousy is not always bad. Sometimes it helps as a motivator to work hard in order to keep pace with others. As a matter of fact, jealousy is the product of a destructive and restless mind. The ill effect of jealousy comes when it is impure and one starts cursing thereby causing heartburn. The worst form of jealousy is when a person starts having an urge to degrade the other person painting out his defects through backbiting and scandal mongering. A jealous man not only feels a burning sensation in his heart but starts serious planning in order to harm the person. A jealous person is in a state of obsession with the idea that other person's very existence is a source of misery and a threat to his happiness. Jealousy may also sometimes lead to destroying, hurting or removing the other person from his way.

Jealousy is the worst enemy

You have come to a stage when you are retiring, looking for spirituality and wisdom for peace. You have witnessed various kinds of jealousy in your long life and I have no doubt that you are aware that jealousy is associated with many negative traits of personality. It makes the person fraudulent and insincere with the people around him. You must have observed in your working life that jealousy promotes anger, cruelty, hatred and pride. A person who is of jealous mind is deprived of cosmic love. The energy and vitality of the person goes away. The ramifications of jealousy are not only confined to your working life but they also destroy the harmony among family members, friends and neighbours. If I am allows to enlarge the ill effects of jealousy then I must say that it is one of the greatest enemies of culture and progress among human beings around the world. It has ruined many homes, frustrated the hopes and broken many hearts.

You all know the ill effects of jealousy. Let's see how we can remove this feeling. Knowing that it is a vice obstructing the peace of mind taking us away from spirituality. Let us understand the root cause of jealousy. It is a complex mental process that arises in the mind which has been degraded due to wastage of will power. One may feel that external objects of persons are responsible for creating jealousy in the heart. But it is not true. One is afflicted with jealousy because he is dissatisfied with himself and he is not living life of enrichment. In fact, the inner unrest renders the mind amenable to psychological diseases and jealousy is one of them. In some of the cases jealousy is based on illusions because what you think to be true of another person's situation may not be the same in reality.

The best way of overcoming jealousy is to acquire soul realization, since all souls are of the same composition. The idea that other people are so happy and you are miserable is wrong because everyone in this world is placed due to divine creation. If you are not enlightened then it is natural that you will suffer with internal sorrow and restlessness. You must realize that everybody has got his or her own problems and shortcomings and if you really knew the actual condition of the people around then instead of jealousy you would have developed a sense of sympathy and goodwill towards them.

Self-realization is important

Consider a scenario. Two patients suffering from different diseases are admitted in the hospital. One patient is getting delicious dishes for breakfast and the other patient is having a tasteless soup only. Can there be a cause for jealousy? Certainly not, because both the patients understand their condition and their limitation of food intake. It's a matter of self-realization which is not allowing the other patient to feel jealous. At very high level of cosmic perspective, again I may advocate the ideal of seeing oneself as a cosmic being and not as an individual looking at all personalities as manifestation of the same self. It will give you the feeling that every human being in this world is like your child or near relative. This will make you satisfied. You would feel they deserve great joy and their happiness is yours. The world will look like your family, a part of your body. *"You know that your nose is never jealous of your eyes because the eyes are spherical and nose is conical."* Each part of your body performs its functions in relations to the organic unity of the whole. Therefore, it should not be difficult for you to believe that every person is related to the organic whole of the universe and has got his or her role in it clearly defined. It is for you to fulfill the role selflessly and mould your destiny to heart's desire.

Take another situation when you see a person threatening your progress then you must realize he is not in your way. No one can obstruct you. You are as free and separate as the distant stars. Feel as if you are the spirit and your freedom is endless. It is you and you only, who is responsible for shaping your destiny according the thoughts and actions. Therefore, no other person, can be an impediment in your path. When you feel jealous, instead of weakening your will by sustaining the fuel of jealousy in your heart, you should try to promote self effort to better your circumstances.

Lastly, I must emphasize that your efforts and good deeds are the real strengths. And if any situation invokes jealousy, you must constantly think about that person linking your efforts and deeds with the deeds and efforts of that person. Finally, if you want to come out of jealous situation you must feel that person close to you and you will start loving that person unconditionally overlooking any deficiency in his personality. Try to reach out and serve the higher aspect of the person that you are jealous of. I mean to say that if you feel jealous towards a person serve that person instead of trying to bring him down through sabotage or suppress him. When you try to suppress a person you degrade both yourself and the person concerned. Whereas, by serving the same person you raise your sentiments which would make you realize that you had no reason to be jealous. Rather you will develop a spirit of charity and magnanimity. Believe me a situation will come that by seeing that person more prosperous than you, you will feel delighted as if, he is your brother who is doing good in life. The yoga philosophy also teaches that all human beings are linked to the universal ocean of life. We all are children of divine self.

I would like to conclude the remedy for this vice by saying that when you hear the great achievement made by others do not allow the burning sensation of jealousy in you. Rather feel that what other person has done you can also do. Do not look for the defects of the other person rather look for positive qualities to emulate. This will make you unfold your own latent talents. You will enrich your personality by eradicating the menace of jealousy through which you will feel immense freedom and get powerful life. Your love and compassion will make you overcome the inflated ego and you will get inspiration from the people who are successful.

Let me divide the word 'jealousy' to develop a new word "zeal – ousy". Meaning thereby 'zeal' to evolve, zeal to become a noble person, zeal to become enlighted and 'oust' wherein all negative quality will disappear forever.

Waxing and waning of the mind

We have discussed the six vices which come in the way of mental peace throughout our life. Elimination of these vices is very important for a person who is retiring. If you go deep into genesis of these vices you will observe that their root cause is desire. If it is not fulfilled, it turns into craving and craving turns into mental confusions and it continues to form diverse impressions in our subconscious mind. These would colour our experiences. All these deposit in the form of impressions in unconscious depth of a person's mind. The realities of a person's day-to-day life cycle in his mind. The cycle of mind revolves around desires, actions, experiences, impressions, subtle desires and thought waves. All these attributes touch each other and move like a cycle. We need to control the movement and intensity of each of these.

Patience is the key to success

We discussed about various vices and their causes and remedies. In fact desire, anger, greed, pride, delusion and jealousy, these all are impurities which exist in your mind like clouds. *"However, you have the sun in your mind to help in fight against these clouds."* These impurities will not stay for long if you are able to recognize your spirit as a soul which is pure. Let me tell you that you must have the power of observing your mind to detect when these impure emotions emerge. Be alert and watch for the clouds of impurities and look for dissolving them. Your negative emotions are all by-products of non-fulfillment of your inner aspirations. Don't ignore them, recognize their existence because they have the purposeful role to play. At the same time be careful that you must move on. You need to struggle with the mental impurities in meaningful manner to control and gradually eliminate them.

Patience is the key word to observe, understand and fight with the inner impurities. In the process, you will see that impure thoughts and feelings do not find expressions in your speech and action. Believe me that the best philosophy is to love through patience. It is the love for God at all times. You allow your mind to be joyous it will not give chance for negative thoughts to develop. In any case, whenever negative feelings develop then do the same way as told earlier. Your experiences of joy, happiness and sadness are related to the impressions of your unconscious mind. Let your spirit be high with patience and love which will make your mind joyful. At times, you will find that your mind is struggling with many thoughts and your inner soul is busy in lively discussion with those thoughts–negative and positive. The world around you may be in silence but inside the mind there is so much noise instead of peace. Do not allow conflicting thoughts to emerge, which agitate the mind.

Take the example of a swan, swimming in water but when the swan decides to fly it shakes off the water particles and flies away. You should perform the same while doing your duty. The moment you come out shake off all your tensions and worries and relax in the arm of the Almighty God. The arms of God are there within you. Your thoughts should be like a still water of the lake without waves. Meditation is the best exercise to achieve this kind of pure feelings in the mind.

Finally, I would like to say that you must develop the quality of observing and grasping the positive thoughts of others so as to distract from negative qualities of others. Constantly looking at others, errors and faults may make your mind bitter but you need to understand that it hurts you only whenever you focus on negative thoughts about others. You are not realizing that by thinking negative about others, finding faults in others, so much negativity is inhaled in your mind which is getting stored in your unconscious mind. You need to change your attitude in such situations so that you filter the negative things which are being grasped by you. Look at person always in a positive manner and realize that God is shining through his or her eyes. I am not saying that appreciate the bad persons but just for something in everyone which can be admired.

Always remember that when your mind is filled with the vices of anger, hate, greed and passion, the spirit in you turns away from the divine self. This would increase the distance between you and your soul. On the other hand, if your mind is filled with love, affection, contentment and other divine virtues the distance will be shortened. It has been rightly said, "You take one step towards God and God takes one hundred steps towards you." Believe me when your mind shines with purity there cannot be any distance between you and your inner self because you will be seeing the things with the clear mind through self realization and soul awareness speeds up your freedom from cycles of birth and death.

Transform your personality

You have seen many decades of life and now are nearing the age of retirement, you are looking for change in your external habits, reaction and values, but you are not transformed, you remain the same person with similar cravings and weaknesses with vices. If you are looking for peace, you need to bring about a transformation in the inner nature. Integral yoga develops personality because spiritual understanding is like a philosopher's stone that has got the capacity to change the basic metal of human desires into shining gold of spiritual aspirations. Integration of personality and transformation of inner life are the important aspects of spirituality.

Yoga comes quite handy in achieving the goal by way of meditation, devotion, action and wisdom in daily life. The results of practicing yoga are well evident, since it outgrows your temptation, weakness and delusions. Yoga is not just exercises as some people believe. Though exercises are necessary to keep you healthy, it is there in yoga in the form of various postures which can be practised depending upon the flexibility of your body as we have discussed under the health management. Yoga makes you to discover yourself. You get the knowledge within yourself that you are not this body, mind and senses but you are the spirit which is pure without any vices. You are there not only to listen but also to meditate and reflect the essential nature what you possess and require to be asserted by elevating the mind. Why you should entertain the feelings and thoughts which are degrading you and the desires which make you to humiliate. Always go away from the concepts of life that are based on ignorance. Believe that moulding of destiny is in your hand. You are the architect of your life. The peace is not far away, it is only a matter of making efforts to achieve the same.

Another form of yoga is selfless service which teaches you to get involved in *karma* yoga which helps to purify and inspire in moulding your destiny. It will remove the clouds of negative sentiments by giving the feeling of realization that the things that created anger, hate and jealousy in your mind are rather meaningless. The devotion is also a form of yoga because as you pray to God and practise *mantras* it automatically develops awareness towards divine love for purifying and giving strength to your mind. This sweetness of divine love washes all impurities whether it is greed, hatred, anger or jealousy.

You must be thinking that when I talked about three loves there was no mention of love to God. But it is not so because self-purification and awareness go a long way for the love of God. Your love for the people will not be complete because of impurities of selfishness and attachment, therefore, it is necessary to understand that God is the innermost source of love and this divine love is always there in the heart. It is the security of faith which does not come and go it never gets exhausted. The divine love gives sweetness to life and strength to mind.

Don't be in a hurry. Have patience. The spirituality and wisdom for peace will come slowly as you move towards the right direction. Don't be like a person who was going with the torch in the night thinking that how he will go miles to complete the journey with the torch which can illuminate only few yards. One has to realize that if the torch is in your hand it will keep on illuminating the path as you go ahead. Similarly, for attaining spiritualism you must keep the torch of divine love in your hands.

Remember that fear always lurks behind perfectionism. Confronting your fears and allowing yourself the right to be human can, paradoxically, make you a far happier and more productive person.

Let us get inspired

- Don't say you don't have enough time. You have exactly the same number of hours per day that were given to Mahatma Gandhi, Mother Teresa, Gurudeva Rabindranath Tagore and Albert Einstein.
- The bad news is time flies. The good news is you're the pilot.
- A wise person does at once, what a fool does at last. Both do the same thing, only at different times.
- Many people seem to think that success in one area can compensate for failure in the other areas. But can it really...? True effectiveness requires balance.
- Never let yesterday use up today.

Food for thoughts

- One worthwhile task carried to a successful conclusion is worth half-a-hundred half finished tasks.
- To think too long about doing a thing often becomes its undoing.
- A year from now you will you had started today.

- The surest way to be late is to have plenty of time.
- What you meet in life is fixed but how meet is in your hands.

Quotes to remember

- Obstacles are those frightful things you see when you take your eyes off your goal.
- Heaven on earth is a choice you must make, not a place we must find.
- Always bear in mind that your own resolution to succeed is more important than any other thing.
- The only limit to our realizations of tomorrow will be our doubts of today.
- It's never too late to be what you might have been.
- No one can cheat you out of ultimate success but yourself.
- More men fail through lack of purpose than lack of talent.

Only one chance

Sometimes you get only one chance!

One chance to put aside your pride and say humbly, "I was wrong," or "It was all my fault," or even, "We were both foolish."

One chance to explain a misunderstanding that, if ignored, would sour a friendship.

One chance to hear what another needs to tell you.

One chance to defend a friend when slighting remarks are made against him.

One chance to accept a shy but sincere offer of friendship.

One chance to stand up and be counted when you don't agree with the crowd.

One chance to say, "No" when it is important to say "No", but easier to say "Yes".

One chance to refuse to be talked into doing something you know you shouldn't.

One chance to right a wrong you've done.

Once chance to choose the right road when you come to crossroads in your life.

One chance to stand up and face a hard situation instead of running away from it.

Sometimes you get only that once chance!

THE MAINTENANCE AND WELFARE OF PARENTS AND SENIOR CITIZENS ACT, 2007

AN

ACT

to provide for more effective provisions for the maintenance and welfare of parents and senior citizens guaranteed and recognized under the Constitution and for matters connected therewith or incidental thereto.

Be it enacted by Parliament in the Fifty-eighth Year of the Republic of India as follows :

CHAPTER 1
PRELIMINARY

1. Short title, Extent, Application and commencement:

(1) This Act may be called the Maintenance and Welfare of Parents and Senior Citizens Act, 2007.

(2) It extends to the whole of India except the State of Jammu and Kashmir and it applies also to citizens of India outside India.

(3) It shall come into force in a State on such date as the State Government may, by notification

in the Official Gazette, appoint.

2. Definitions : In this Act, unless the context otherwise requires,—

(a) "children" includes son, daughter, grandson and granddaughter but does not include a minor;

(b) "maintenance" includes provision for food, clothing, residence and medical attendance and treatment;

(c) "minor" means a person who, under the provisions of the Indian Majority Act, 1875, (9 of 1875) is deemed not to have attained the age of majority;

(d) "parent" means father or mother whether biological, adoptive or step father or step mother, as the case may be, whether or not the father or the mother is a senior citizen;

(e) "prescribed" means prescribed by rules made by the State Government under this Act;

(f) "property" means property of any kind, whether movable or immovable, ancestral or self-acquired, tangible or intangible and includes rights or interests in such property;

(g) "relative" means any legal heir of the childless senior citizen who is not a minor and is in possession of or would inherit his property after his death;

(h) "senior citizen" means any person being a citizen of India, who has attained the age of sixty years or above;

(i) "State Government", in relation to a Union territory, means the administrator thereof appointed under article 239 of the Constitution;

(j) "Tribunal" means the Maintenance Tribunal

constituted under section 7;

(k) "welfare" means provision for food, health care, recreation centres and other amenities necessary for the senior citizens.

3. Act to have overriding effect : The provisions of this Act shall have effect notwithstanding anything inconsistent therewith contained in any enactment other than this Act, or in any instrument having effect by virtue of any enactment other than this Act.

CHAPTER II
MAINTENANCE OF PARENTS AND SENIOR CITIZENS

4. Maintenance of parents and senior citizens :

(1) A senior citizen including parent who is unable to maintain himself from his own earning or out of the property owned by him, shall be entitled to make an application under section 5 in case of—

(i) parent or grand-parent, against one or more of his children not being a minor;

(ii) a childless senior citizen, against such of his relative referred to in clause (g) of section 2.

(2) The obligation of the children or relative, as the case may be, to maintain a senior citizen extends to the needs of such citizen so that senior citizen may lead a normal life.

(3) The obligation of the children to maintain his or her parent extends to the needs of such parent either father or mother or both, as the case may

be, so that such parent may lead a normal life.

(4) Any person being a relative of a senior citizen and having sufficient means shall maintain such senior citizen provided he is in possession of the property of such senior citizen or he would inherit the property of such senior citizen:

Provided that where more than one relatives are entitled to inherit the property of a senior citizen, the maintenance shall be payable by such relative in the proportion in which they would inherit his property.

5. Application for maintenance :

(1) An application for maintenance under section 4, may be made—

(a) by a senior citizen or a parent, as the case may be; or

(b) if he is incapable, by any other person or organisation authorised by him; or

(c) the Tribunal may take cognizance suo motu.

Explanation.- For the purposes of this section "organisation" means any voluntary association registered under the Societies Registration Act, 1860, (21 of 1860) or any other law for the time being in force.

(2) The Tribunal may, during the pendency of the proceeding regarding monthly allowance for the maintenance under this section, order such children or relative to make a monthly allowance for the interim maintenance of such senior citizen including parent and to pay the same to such senior citizen including parent as the Tribunal may from time to time direct.

(3) On receipt of an application for maintenance under sub-section (1) after giving notice of the application to the children or relative and after giving the parties an opportunity of being heard, hold an inquiry for determining the amount of maintenance.

(4) An application filed under sub-section (2) for the monthly allowance for the maintenance and expenses for proceeding shall be disposed of within ninety days from the date of the service of notice of the application to such person:

Provided that the Tribunal may extend the said period, once for a maximum period of thirty days in exceptional circumstances for reasons to be recorded in writing.

(5) An application for maintenance under sub-section (1) may be filed against one or more persons:

Provided that such children or relative may implead the other person liable to maintain parent in the application for maintenance.

(6) Where a maintenance order was made against more than one person, the death of one of them does not affect the liability of others to continue paying maintenance.

(7) Any such allowance for the maintenance and expenses for proceeding shall be payable from the date of the order, or, if so ordered, from the date of the application for maintenance or expenses of proceeding, as the case may be.

(8) If, children or relative so ordered fail, without sufficient cause to comply with the order, any

such Tribunal may, for every breach of the order, issue a warrant for levying the amount due in the manner provided for levying fines, and may sentence such person for the whole, or any part of each month's allowance for the maintenance and expenses of proceeding, as the case may be, remaining unpaid after the execution of the warrant, to imprisonment for a term which may extend to one month or until payment if sooner made whichever is earlier:

Provided that no warrant shall be issued for the recovery of any amount due under this section unless application be made to the Tribunal to levy such amount within a period of three months from the date on which it became due.

6. Jurisdiction and procedure :

(1) The proceedings under section 5 may be taken against any children or relative in any district—

(a) where he resides or last resided; or

(b) where children or relative resides.

(2) On receipt of the application under section 5, the Tribunal shall issue a process for procuring the presence of children or relative against whom the application is filed.

(3) For securing the attendance of children or relative the Tribunal shall have the power of a Judicial Magistrate of first class as provided under the Code of Criminal Procedure, 1973. (2 of 1974)

(4) All evidence to such proceedings shall be taken in the presence of the children or relative against whom an order for payment

of maintenance is proposed to be made, and shall be recorded in the manner prescribed for summons cases:

Provided that if the Tribunal is satisfied that the children or relative against whom an order for payment of maintenance is proposed to be made is wilfully avoiding service, or wilfully neglecting to attend the Tribunal, the Tribunal may proceed to hear and determine the case ex parte.

(5) Where the children or relative is residing out of India, the summons shall be served by the Tribunal through such authority, as the Central Government may by notification in the official Gazette, specify in this behalf.

(6) The Tribunal before hearing an application under section 5 may, refer the same to a Conciliation Officer and such Conciliation Officer shall submit his findings within one month and if amicable settlement has been arrived at, the Tribunal shall pass an order to that effect.

Explanation.- For the purposes of this sub-section "Conciliation Officer" means any person or representative of an organisation referred to in Explanation to sub-section (1) of section 5 or the Maintenance Officers designated by the State Government under subsection (1) of section 18 or any other person nominated by the Tribunal for this purpose.

7. Constitution of Maintenance Tribunal :

(1) The State Government shall within a period of six months from the date of the commencement of this Act, by notification in

the Official Gazette, constitute for each Subdivision one or more Tribunals as may be specified in the notification for the purpose of adjudicating and deciding upon the order for maintenance under section 5.

(2) The Tribunal shall be presided over by an officer not below the rank of Sub-Divisional Officer of a State.

(3) Where two or more Tribunals are constituted for any area, the State Government may, by general or special order, regulate the distribution of business among them.

8. Summary procedure in case of inquiry :

(1) In holding any inquiry under section 5, the Tribunal may, subject to any rules that may be prescribed by the State Government in this behalf, follow such summary procedure as it deems fit.

(2) The Tribunal shall have all the powers of a Civil Court for the purpose of taking evidence on oath and of enforcing the attendance of witnesses and of compelling the discovery and production of documents and material objects and for such other purposes as may be prescribed; and the Tribunal shall be deemed to be a Civil Court for all the purposes of section 195 and Chapter XXVI of the Code of Criminal Procedure, 1973. (2 of 1974)

(3) Subject to any rule that may be made in this behalf, the Tribunal may, for the purpose of adjudicating and deciding upon any claim for maintenance, choose one or more persons possessing special knowledge of any matter

relevant to the inquiry to assist it in holding the inquiry.

9. Order for maintenance:
   (1) If children or relatives, as the case may be, neglect or refuse to maintain a senior citizen being unable to maintain himself, the Tribunal may, on being satisfied of such neglect or refusal, order such children or relatives to make a monthly allowance at such monthly rate for the maintenance of such senior citizen, as the Tribunal may deem fit and to pay the same to such senior citizen as the Tribunal may, from time to time, direct.
   (2) The maximum maintenance allowance which may be ordered by such Tribunal shall be such as may be prescribed by the State Government which shall not exceed ten thousand rupees per month.
10. Alteration in allowance:
   (1) On proof of misrepresentation or mistake of fact or a change in the circumstances of any person, receiving a monthly allowance under section 9, for the maintenance ordered under that section to pay a monthly allowance for the maintenance, the Tribunal may make such alteration, as it thinks fit, in the allowance for the maintenance.
   (2) Where it appears to the Tribunal that, in consequence of any decision of a competent Civil Court, any order made under section 9 should be cancelled or varied, it shall cancel the order or, as the case may be, vary the same accordingly.

11. Enforcement of order of maintenance:

(1) A copy or the order of maintenance and including the order regarding expenses of proceedings, as the case may be, shall be given without payment of any fee to the senior citizen or to parent, as the case may be, in whose favour it is made and such order may be enforced by any Tribunal in any place where the person against whom it is made, such Tribunal on being satisfied as to the identity of the parties and the non-payment of the allowance, or as the case may be, expenses, due.

(2) A maintenance order made under this Act shall have the same force and effect as an order passed under Chapter IX of the Code of Criminal Procedure, 1973 (2 of 1974) and shall be executed in the manner prescribed for the execution of such order by that Code.

12. Option regarding maintenance in certain cases : Notwithstanding anything contained in Chapter IX of the Code of Criminal Procedure, 1973 (2 of 1974) where a senior citizen or a parent is entitled for maintenance under the said Chapter and also entitled for maintenance under this Act may, without prejudice to the provisions of Chapter IX of the said Code, claim such maintenance under either of those Acts but not under both.

13. Deposit of maintenance amount : When an order is made under this Chapter, the children or relative who is required to pay any amount in terms of such order shall, within thirty days of the date of announcing the order by the Tribunal, deposit the

entire amount ordered in such manner as the Tribunal may direct.

14. Award of interest where any claim is allowed : Where any Tribunal makes an order for maintenance made under this Act, such Tribunal may direct that in addition to the amount of maintenance, simple interest shall also be paid at such rate and from such date not earlier than the date of making the application as may be determined by the Tribunal which shall not be less than five per cent, and not more than eighteen per cent:

    Provided that where any application for maintenance under Chapter IX of the Code of Criminal Procedure, 1973 (2 of 1974) is pending before a Court at the commencement of this Act, then the Court shall allow the withdrawal of such application on the request of the parent and such parent shall be entitled to file an application for maintenance before the Tribunal.

15. Constitution of Appellate Tribunal:
    (1) The State Government may, by notification in the Official Gazette, constitute one Appellate Tribunal for each district to hear the appeal against the order of the Tribunal.
    (2) The Appellate Tribunal shall be presided over by an officer not below the rank of District Magistrate.

16. Appeals:
    (1) Any senior citizen or a parent, as the case may be, aggrieved by an order of a Tribunal may, within sixty days from the date of the order, prefer an appeal to the Appellate Tribunal:

Provided that on appeal, the children or relative who is required to pay any amount in terms of such maintenance order shall continue to pay to such parent the amount so ordered, in the manner directed by the Appellate Tribunal:

Provided further that the Appellate Tribunal may, entertain the appeal after the expiry of the said period of sixty days, if it is satisfied that the appellant was prevented by sufficient cause from preferring the appeal in time.

(2) On receipt of an appeal, the Appellate Tribunal shall, cause a notice to be served upon the respondent.

(3) The Appellate Tribunal may call for the record of proceedings from the Tribunal against whose order the appeal is preferred.

(4) The Appellate Tribunal may, after examining the appeal and the records called for, either allow or reject the appeal.

(5) The Appellate Tribunal shall, adjudicate and decide upon the appeal filed against the order of the Tribunal and the order of the Appellate Tribunal shall be final:

Provided that no appeal shall be rejected unless an opportunity has been given to both the parties of being heard in person or through a duly authorised representative.

(6) The Appellate Tribunal shall make an endeavour to pronounce its order in writing within one month of the receipt of an appeal.

(7) A copy of every order made under sub-section (5) shall be sent to both the parties free of cost.

17. Right to legal representation : Notwithstanding

anything contained in any law, no party to a proceeding before a Tribunal or Appellate Tribunal shall be represented by a legal practitioner.

18. Maintenance Officer :

(1) The State Government shall designate the District Social Welfare Officer or an officer not below the rank of a District Social Welfare Officer, by whatever name called as Maintenance Officer.

(2) The Maintenance Officer referred to in sub-section (1), shall represent a parent if he so desires, during the proceedings of the Tribunal, or the Appellate Tribunal, as the case may be.

CHAPTER III
ESTABLISHMENT OF OLDAGE HOMES

19. Establishment of oldage homes :

(1) The State Government may establish and maintain such number of oldage homes at accessible places, as it may deem necessary, in a phased manner, beginning with at least one in each district to accommodate in such homes a minimum of one hundred fifty senior citizens who are indigent.

(2) The State Government may, prescribe a scheme for management of oldage homes, including the standards and various types of services to be provided by them which are necessary for medical care and means of entertainment to the inhabitants of such homes.

Explanation.-For the purposes of this section,

"indigent" means any senior citizen who is not having sufficient means, as determined by the State Government, from time to time, to maintain himself.

CHAPTER IV
PROVISIONS FOR MEDICAL CARE OF SENIOR CITIZEN

20. Medical support for senior citizen : The State Government shall ensure that, -
   (i) the Government hospitals or hospitals funded fully or partially by the Government shall provide beds for all senior citizens as far as possible;
   (ii) separate queues be arranged for senior citizens;
   (iii) facility for treatment of chronic, terminal and degenerative diseases is expanded for senior citizens;
   (iv) research activities for chronic elderly diseases and ageing is expanded;
   (v) there are earmarked facilities for geriatric patients in every district hospital duly headed by a medical officer with experience in geriatric care.

CHAPTER V
PROTECTION OF LIFE AND PROPERTY OF SENIOR CITIZEN

21. Measures for publicity awareness, etc., for welfare of senior citizen : The State Government shall, take all measures to ensure that—
   (i) the provisions of this Act are given wide

publicity through public media including the television, radio and the print, at regular intervals;

(ii) the Central Government and State Government Officers, including the police officers and the members of the judicial service, are given periodic sensitization and awareness training on the issues relating to this Act;

(iii) effective co-ordination between the services provided by the concerned Ministries or Departments dealing with law, home affairs, health and welfare, to address the issues relating to the welfare of the senior citizens and periodical review of the same is conducted.

22. Authorities who may be specified for implementing the provisions of this Act :

(1) The State Government may, confer such powers and impose such duties on a District Magistrate as may be necessary, to ensure that the provisions of this Act are properly carried out and the District Magistrate may specify the officer, subordinate to him, who shall exercise all or any of the powers, and perform all or any of the duties, so conferred or imposed and the local limits within which such powers or duties shall be carried out by the officer as may be prescribed.

(2) The State Government shall prescribe a comprehensive action plan for providing protection of life and property of senior citizens.

23. Transfer of property to be void in certain circumstances :

(1) Where any senior citizen who, after the commencement of this Act, has transferred by way of gift or otherwise, his property, subject to the condition that the transferee shall provide the basic amenities and basic physical needs to the transferor and such transferee refuses or fails to provide such amenities and physical needs, the said transfer of property shall be deemed to have been made by fraud or coercion or under undue influence and shall at the option of the transferor be declared void by the Tribunal.

(2) Where any senior citizen has a right to receive maintenance out of an estate and such estate or part thereof is transferred, the right to receive maintenance may be enforced against the transferee if the transferee has notice of the right, or if the transfer is gratuitous; but not against the transferee for consideration and without notice of right.

(3) If, any senior citizen is incapable of enforcing the rights under sub-sections (1) and (2), action may be taken on his behalf by any of the organisation referred to in Explanation to sub-section (1) of section 5.

CHAPTER VI
OFFENCES AND PROCEDURE FOR TRIAL

24. Exposure and abandonment of senior citizen : Whoever, having the care or protection of senior citizen leaves, such senior citizen in any place with the intention of wholly abandoning such

senior citizen, shall be punishable with imprisonment of either description for a term which may extend to three months or fine which may extend to five thousand rupees or with both.

25. Cognizance of offences:

(1) Notwithstanding anything contained in the Code of Criminal Procedure, 1973, (2 of 1974) every offence under this Act shall be cognizable and bailable.

(2) An offence under this Act shall be tried summarily by a Magistrate.

CHAPTER VII
MISCELLANEOUS

26. Officers to be public servants: Every officer or staff appointed to exercise functions under this Act shall be deemed to be a public servant within the meaning of section 21 (45 of 1860) of the Indian Penal Code.

27. Jurisdiction of civil courts barred : No Civil Court shall have jurisdiction in respect of any matter to which any provision of this Act applies and no injunction shall be granted by any Civil Court in respect of anything which is done or intended to be done by or under this Act.

28. Protection of action taken in good faith : No suit, prosecution or other legal proceeding shall lie against the Central Government, the State Governments or the local authority or any officer of the Government in respect of anything which is done in good faith or intended to be done in pursuance of this Act and any rules or orders

made thereunder.

29. Power to remove difficulties: If any difficulty arises in giving effect to the provisions of this Act, the State Government may, by order published in the Official Gazette, make such provisions not inconsistent with the provisions of this Act, as appear to it to be necessary or expedient for removing the difficulty:

Provided that no such order shall be made after the expiry of a period of two years from the date of the commencement of this Act.

30. Power of Central Government to give directions: The Central Government may give directions to State Governments as to the carrying into execution of the provisions of this Act.

31. Power of Central Government to review: The Central Government may make periodic review and monitor the progress of the implementation of the provisions of this Act by the State Governments.

32. Power of State Government to make rules:

(1) The State Government may, by notification in the Official Gazette, make rules for carrying out the purposes of this Act.

(2) Without prejudice to the generality of the foregoing power, such rules may provide for—

(a) the manner of holding inquiry under section 5 subject to such rules as may be prescribed under sub-section (1) of section 8;

(b) the power and procedure of the Tribunal for other purposes under subsection (2) of section 8;

(c) the maximum maintenance allowance which may be ordered by the Tribunal under sub-section (2) of section 9;

(d) the scheme for management of oldage homes, including the standards and various types of services to be provided by them which are necessary for medical care and means of entertainment to the inhabitants of such homes under sub-section (2) of section 19;

(e) the powers and duties of the authorities for implementing the provisions of this Act, under sub-section (1) of section 22;

(f) a comprehensive action plan for providing protection of life and property of senior citizens under sub-section (2) of section 22;

(g) any other matter which is to be, or may be, prescribed.

(3) Every rule made under this Act shall be laid, as soon as may be after it is made, before each House of State Legislature, where it consists of two houses or where such legislature consists of one House, before that House.

●●●